P9-BZI-880

ADVANCE PRAISE FOR
FROM NEWTON, EINSTEIN TO GOD

"Dr. Leong Ying possesses the rare storyteller's ability to make virtually any subject both lucid and compelling. Though this is a personal memoir about his family and their struggle with poverty, behind it is a bigger story concerning the cultural divide in Singapore, Great Britain, and the United States. Facing many obstacles, Dr. Ying finally achieved his dream of becoming a nuclear scientist and remained determined to discover a new theory about the universe. This book, *From Newton, Einstein to GOD*, is a case in point."

—Christine Choy, *Professor, Tisch School of Arts,*
Oscar-nominated Director

"Leong has been involved in fundraising events for my Shoe4Africa organization, including joining our team for the New York marathon. The stories of his spiritual awakening are a most enthralling tale, and one that I have recognized through my own near-death experience. His poetic words are not just beautiful, but have significant meaning that will resonate powerfully with the readers."

—Toby Tanser, *Founder, Shoe4Africa*

"Dr. Leong Ying's groundbreaking work to expand the consciousness of the planet is unsurpassed. I have personally known him for over a decade, and during that time he has continued to persevere with his passion for writing. Having deep insights into the religious, spiritual, and scientific arcs that continue to inspire great thinkers to dig more deeply into the meaning of life, Dr. Ying's views and insights must be taken seriously. I have believed in his theories for some time now. Having written a best-selling memoir about my life that is in production as a feature film written by Terence Winter (*Wolf of Wall Street, Boardwalk Empire, The Sopranos*), I have been touched very deeply by Dr. Ying's work, his beliefs, and his way of looking at the world. I commend his commitment to and the completion of this long-awaited study of an important aspect of his purpose."

—Tod Volpe, *CEO, Truth is Cool!*

"Dr. Ying's second book, *From Newton, Einstein to GOD*, is going to be another milestone of his life's journey in the quest to find the true sense of one's life in the duality space—the twin universes. This poetic family memoir is the mirror reflecting his inner and outer life—the past period and the future that lay ahead, which is vividly reflected in this book."

—Professor Bhadra Man Tuladhar, *founding member, Kathmandu University, Nepal*

FROM NEWTON, EINSTEIN TO GOD

FROM NEWTON, EINSTEIN TO GOD

A POETIC MEMOIR

LEONG YING

EMERALD
BOOK CO.

Published by Emerald Book Company
Austin, TX
www.emeraldbookcompany.com

Distributed by Emerald Book Company

For ordering information or special discounts for bulk purchases, please contact
Emerald Book Company at PO Box 91869, Austin, TX 78709, 512.891.6100.

Design and composition by Greenleaf Book Group
Cover design by Greenleaf Book Group
Cover illustration is taken from an oil painting by Jennie Yip entitled "Mother and Son"

Cataloging-in-Publication data

ISBN 13: 978-1-937110-71-0

Part of the Tree Neutral® program, which offsets the number of trees
consumed in the production and printing of this book by taking proactive
steps, such as planting trees in direct proportion to the number of trees
used: www.treeneutral.com

14 15 16 17 18 19   10 9 8 7 6 5 4 3 2 1

First Edition

Other Edition(s)
eBook ISBN: 978-1-937110-72-7

CONTENTS

IN THE BEGINNING

(1961-1968)

Too young to sense even my own age, it could have been two.

Stood in front of the mirror, contemplating walking through.

Naked, only in brown pants, with scissors in right hand.

To step into the other realm I had to stick the blades in if I can.

Wanting to pop in, just my head, to bring back to family a message.

Though I knew not of death, I sensed it would be a one-way passage.

Still I am unsure what happened that fateful day as I write these verses.

What I am certain is that was the beginning of my adventures with twin universes.

My life began in Singapore, a colonial enclave of the British Empire.

Tropical land of heat that makes even the mad English dogs perspire.

From the birth canal of a native mother of Chinese Fujian ancestry.

And a father who sailed out from Ningbo to serve onboard Her Majesty.

A child knows not of poorness when playing in monsoon waters.

Mindless of adult pains and careless of natural dangers.

Even my entry upon this earth is marked by confusing farce.

Stabbed at Kandang Kerbau hospital by the delivery staff.

The heavens chimed me in before midnight the twenty-sixth of December.

But it is three minutes into the next day before my birth is registered.

I was told I was babysat by my elder sisters

As my mother slaved at work to keep us from hunger.

Small Aunty, Big Aunty, and an uncle with tattoo marks.

This was the Lim clan, with Grandma as the matriarch.

The Ying branch of our family sailed from China,

My father leaving his hometown to seek labor as a minor.

A chef on a merchant vessel plying trade from east to west.

On dock he wedded twice, though my mother was last and best.

First taste of girl was not a pleasant flavor.

She ate a slice of cheese before I kissed her.

To this date I loathe the smelly odor.

Except for grown-up women with fragrant aroma.

Living in a shanty town there was little privacy.

Bedroom lusts and toilet flush were not of quiet niceties.

Even animals of the wild and domestic types

Invaded our opened home without personal invites.

Once I carried in a nest of baby mice.

The screams of horror were not so nice.

We had a dog who didn't seem to like me.

He tried to take a bite that wasn't to be.

My sister jumped in to protect this baby from his hate.

Her bloodied pain meant the end for our pet's fate.

There was a piglet that I did adore.

A playful mate with tasty allure.

Fattened up with scraps of human food.

The night he was butchered saddened my mood.

For the most part I had a happy, carefree childhood.

There was pretense of sadness during a funeral in our neighborhood.

I felt worse for eels my grandma released into freedom during a festive New Year,

Only for bad boys to stone the slippery fishes, which brought on real tears.

Come to think of it, I seem to have more empathy for beasts than my humankind.

Perhaps because dumb animals are as innocent as an infant mind.

In the botanical gardens we were mocked by monkeys.

Into the protective clutches of my mother did I flee.

On my return as a teen I went in search of the simians.

They had long deserted their lush green dominion.

In solemn reflection I recognized that it was to be a futile search.

That day of motherly bond could not be rediscovered on a leafy perch.

A true parent's devotion for their offspring will never waver.

It is within a rebellious child that emotions can taper.

My continued hunt for redemption is fiercely determined.

Hoping one day I will be nursed back to my mother in Eden.

Stories told of past histories I plugged my ears and glazed my eyes.

When one is young you look to the future and up at the skies.

As years passed by, the reality is what came before will show the signs forward.

So now I retrace in these poetic verses the steps of my life backward.

Childhood pranks were one of my specialties.

Bricking up a car's rear wheels to observe its causality.

Most mischievous deeds were experiments upon me.

Cutting my own hair drew mother's anger from which I flee.

Fascinated to see what effects of chewing gum on facial hair.

I manage to bald one side of my eyebrows so it was no longer a pair.

My worst injuries came from a firework explosion.

A nosy face near a buried cracker is not a smart exploration.

If curiosity can indeed kill a cat,

Then my nine lives have already been whacked.

Being near the equator meant seasonal change was from hot to very hot.

Excessive heat was compounded by humidity, making it an uncomfortable spot.

Coolness came from sporadic downpours as skies darkened to dump buckets of rain.

You only had to stand a few minutes in the returning sun to dry out your mane.

My favorite time of year came with the monsoons that flooded the land.

Wading in torrents, joyfully oblivious of the dangers with your life in God's hand.

If the weather was not to my liking, that could not be said of the delicious food.

Most famous local dish is Singaporean chilly crab, a taste that went beyond good.

Influence from Indian, Chinese, and Malay gave us the greatest of meals.

Spicy laksa, chicken rice, and satay are just some of the delightful appeals.

Even the desserts could bring a smile to a condemned man's last supper.

Such as ice kacang, coconut jelly, and fruity durian with its overwhelming odor.

We had no kindergarten, or at least none we could afford.

There was primary schooling where I went to be taught.

All I can remember was singing the national anthem each morning.

And playing tough by volunteering to be first to take the needles for vaccine.

Being dyslexic meant my linguistic skills were at very low limits.

With four national languages to be learned, I was labeled stupid.

Perhaps that's why, along with poor scores in testing of learning fundamentals,

I had an impediment of speaking Chinese words during English recitals.

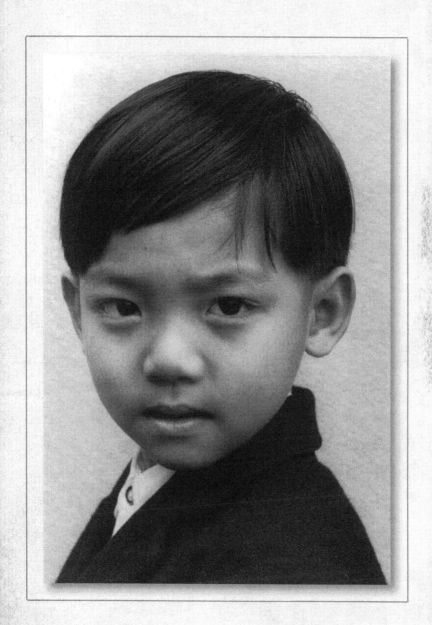

To avoid tropical heat, lessons were early morning to finish
before noon.

It meant many hours of idle play before the rising of the nightly
moon.

My lousy grade card was not a proud thing I wanted to rush
home to show.

So I larked around with cousins and friends until the sun
crept low.

It wasn't all fun in the playground, for once my mate ran onto a
rusty nail.

Rubber sandals on feet offered no protection from being impaled.

Nights were the time for idle gatherings.

Sitting on the cooling porch with siblings.

A favorite hawker comes peddling his yummy congee.

With pot and penny in hand I approach to be greeted fondly.

In later years when I was living in a faraway continent

I gifted cash to my Meals on Wheels server as a compliment.

There were no celebrations for personal anniversaries.

But I never went a day hungry or suffered adversities.

Chinese New Year and Independence Day were festive times.

Floating lighted lanterns on dark waters were highlight primes.

Banquet feasts and opera plays were outdoor events.

A showman, I would dance until my energy was totally vented.

Singapore was ravaged by the Second World War.

Occupied by Japanese Imperial Forces that conquered all.

From China, Korea, Burma they marched south across the strait.

The once-mighty British Empire was on a losing fate.

Evil atrocities on civilians and prisoners were committed upon.

My young mother's haunting experience made her a hater of Nippon.

The end of war brought to the peninsula no peace urgency.

Guerrilla campaign was fought during the Malayan Emergency.

Federation of Malaysia was formed independent of Britannia's rule.

Two years later, on ninth of August 1965, our republic grew.

So I am a baby born into fighting conflicts and peaceful transitions.

Forever I seem to walk down dual paths toward my godly ambitions.

Spiritual veneration in this secular nation is as mixed as its people's ethnic race.

Worshippers of Buddhism, Christianity, Islam, and Hinduism walk at equal pace.

In some cases they even share temples as they read from their different scriptures.

If only the rest of the intolerant world could follow this idyllic picture.

My parents' approach was simply to pay respect to all religions.

Our virtuous paths are forged by our deeds and not our proclamations.

Lim Tua Bak was my mother's full title, born on fourteenth of October 1930.

Parents were Ang Ho Pang and Lim Eng Hock, who worked as a coolie.

Both my grandparents' nationalities are noted as Hokien on the birth registry.

Fujian province in the southeast region of China was their original ancestry.

Though barely five feet off the ground, mum could fight ferociously above her weight.

I recalled baby trotting by her side as she assaulted a guy who towered over her height.

It took many to restrain her as she fought until she was stripped down to her bra.

The wrongdoers who stole money learned the scary way they couldn't run afar.

And even if they did survive my mother's battling assault and vanished,

When story got out, my gangster uncle made sure the guilty were duly punished.

There is a single infant memory I shared with both parents.

For father was absent plying trade on the ocean currents.

Not surprising, therefore, I ran away as I would from a stranger.

And forever in life that marked our ongoing relationship as minor.

Father's Singaporean naturalization had three different names entered in the official book.

He was born in China with the registered names of Soo Huan and Hoong Fook.

But I only knew him by his final designated full title of Ying See Wai.

The multiple variants are how the Chinese dialects are pronounced in different ways.

Like many of his Chinese seaman friends, my dad left the fleet to settle in England.

Most started their new life in the home port of Liverpool when they permanently set foot on land.

Their only skill was cooking so they exchanged the ship's galley for a restaurant kitchen.

A step up in class came when they could buy a business and wear their own boss's apron.

The sixties was a boom time with the local band the Beatles at the pinnacle of global success.

And once my father had his own fish and chip shop, it was time to bring over his entire family nest.

Eldest sister Cher Lee was the first to join our father in the United Kingdom.

I sulked under the bed, refusing to join in the celebration of her newfound freedom.

But it would not be long before it was the turn of mum, me, and sister Kwee Ngin.

It was 1968 when we flew away and into a new chapter of life we were entering.

HOW EDUCATION KILLED
THE SPIRIT

(1968-1993)

Betting on a grey to win the National as a dream-child psychic.

But the straw that killed the camel came from learning physics.

Transformation from natural to manmade was a slow transition.

Innocence of youth overcame by greedy materialistic fixation.

Our new life abroad began in the immigration hall waiting to be processed.

Mum, sis, and little me sat passively for the official's address.

Documents stamped for approval we exited the airport portal.

Driven by dad through a city crazy for its music and football.

Our first English home was in the Liverpool district of Gateacre.

A one-bedroom flat sat above row of shops cramped into half an acre.

The local Scousers refer to our fish and chip shop as a "chippy."

These working-class northerners are renowned for being funny.

We had the corner business premises located at thirty Lee Park Avenue.

Our sleeping quarters directly on top of this source of income revenue.

Side entrances, either side of the shopping precinct, lead into stairwells to the top.

There was a bakery, a newsagent, and a few other stores alongside our shop.

Buses ran along the front of the main road through predominantly a residential route.

So it was busy at lunch, tea, and supper times serving the hungry troops.

Front of our shop had a long serving counter where the customers queued.

We were open daily before noon till midnight with leisurely rest periods few.

Sliced spuds and battered cod were fried in oily lard sizzling in large vats.

Healthy eating was not on the menu, just cheap, tasty grub that would make one fat.

Backyard to the store was a shed where the sacks of potatoes are raped.

A peeling machine would strip off their skin before manually scraped.

This was a duty expected of all family members, including me.

Early in the morning and late at night we still buzz like bumblebees.

The kitchen and bathroom were either side of our upstairs hive.

Two front areas were the lounge and the bedroom that slept five.

Large double windows gave an overhead view of the front road.

An overhanging deck prevents dropping from above any loads.

There were bunk beds and a large bed that I shared with my sisters.

No luxury of air-conditioning or central heating for the cold winters.

Small dining table was against the window next to the television.

While the family worked, the two youngest waited out the daily attrition.

Most of our meals were in the store to which we had to go down.

Sunday the family relaxed together for lunch in Chinatown.

Liverpool had the first Chinatown in Europe dating back to the nineteen century.

Chinese seaman hired by the Blue Funnel Shipping Line establishing a long history.

Trade routes imported silk, cotton, and tea to this northwest English port.

My father served on Her Majesty's merchant fleet even when wars were being fought.

Like many eastern pioneers before him, he settled in this Lancastrian shire.

And here the Chinese community flourished in pursuit of their earthly desires.

Occasionally my dad would take me to the docks to meet his old sailor mates.

Even a small ocean-going merchant vessel is an awesome sight for a kid to take.

As more of his friends came on land to settle, the harbor became a passing landmark.

Only once did he take me to the Chinese seaman club where gambling was on the card.

Mahjong was his sin that my mother hated him for playing.

Any winnings he would spend on his friends who were more than willing.

But when he lost big, it appeared his pals were not equal to the giving.

And worse, he would vent his losing anger at his family without caring.

Fortunately, his partner—my mother—was not one for taking abuse.

She kept hold of the money, giving him only what was for essential use.

My English education started at Belle Vale Infant school.

Most fun learning experience of my life acting the fool.

I'd a hard time learning ABCs, but I already knew my twelve times table.

What I really enjoyed were the piggyback fights, of which I was most capable.

Best friends were Kevin Bacon and Keith Smelley, fondly referred to as Smelly Bacon.

We had a very attractive female teacher who had the boys totally smitten.

But my true desire was for Michelle O'Brien and a cute blonde I can no longer name.

Now I am older I see why my loving gift of a grasshopper turned out to be so lame.

I walked the mile or so from home to school and back.

Biscuit and carton of milk before entering the classroom pack.

Infant schooling was only for a year before graduating to primary.

Though now seven, my tested English language skills were still lousy.

I missed the piggyback games, but the older kids didn't seem to want to ride.

Instead we played rounders, with points scored by each batting side.

But my new favorite playtime activities were marbles and conkers.

One you rolled to hit, and the other you aimed to smash and conquer.

I was the only non-white pupil when I entered the school system at six.

Two years on along came a black kid who doubled the racial mix.

He was tough enough to muscle his way to joint top cock in the pecking order.

I was third-ranking cock until savaged by a girl in a battling furor.

Scathing nails and pulling hair was not a style I'd previously fought in.

That loss taught me a painful lesson you had to do whatever to win.

I'm not sure if my family found out about my girlie beating and loss of mojo.

Or coincidence that soon after I was signed up to the local martial arts dojo.

Judo means "the gentle way," which seems paradoxical for a combat sport.

I hated being thrown to the ground, but at least I was very well taught.

Only once did I burst into tears after suffering a contested defeat.

But soon I rose in the ranks to become a student of steely meat.

I regularly won competitions because I was strong and fast.

Once I even got to the finals of two weight division class.

The lightweight I fought all the way through to win with ease.

In the middleweight final I failed, and to this day I am not pleased.

My real street fighting record is still one defeat to that vicious schoolgirl.

In combats I could put my rivals on the ground with exquisite hurls.

But I was too small in stature to try out for the playground fighter's title.

Big bullies avoided me, for they knew I would scuffle even though I was little.

I was also considered tough for taking on opposing schools in pitch battle.

In reality we threw stones and then ran like cowardly cattle.

One of the nearby rivals was Gateacre Public Comprehensive High School.

The older students included my sister, our eldest sibling already in the working pool.

Cher worked as a server at the front of the counter with a couple of hired hands.

Dishing out fish and chips sprinkled with salt and vinegar from bottled cans.

Bundled in clean white wrapper and then overlay with used newspaper.

Fingers tore the wrappings to feast and satisfy greedy hunger.

Mother controlled the all-important money and the frying pans.

Father relegated to the kitchen, preparing sauces and spam.

The food we served was the average English working man's favorite tastes.

Main meal of the working class was tea-time coming out of the factory gates.

Lunch we catered to stay-home mothers and office pickups riding on their bikes.

Supper was quiet until the drunks staggered out of the pubs for an evening bite.

Sunday we closed and Monday all the local businesses worked half-days.

Hours were brutally long, and our family rarely took vacations to relax and play.

The only family holiday we took was a day's outing to Blackpool seaside resort.

Famous for its tower that looks like a copy of the Eiffel in the French court.

Other attractions were the street illuminations and kiss-me-quick hats.

We had more excitement the day we brought in a pussy cat.

Like the pet dog that tried to savage baby me, kitty didn't last long.

Father cried when told to dump out the feline to be alone.

Our next animal was a chicken we kept in the upstairs kitchen.

My mum brought it to lay fresh eggs to save us pittance.

A single hen could not supply a growing family with yolks.

So, like my former playmate piglet, she became the meal for us folks.

An addition to our ranks came in the shape of my brother Peter.

So the story was told that my mother wanted to name him Beatles.

It doesn't even rhyme with the famous Fab Four band.

Luckily the registrar picked a more common name with his own hand.

Otherwise, imagine the abuse he would go through life with such a name.

Although he could be labeled as the fifth Beatle to add to his fame.

My youngest sister and I were often left to nurse the new baby.

For an eight-year-old I was surprisingly good at changing nappy.

There were no disposables and we had to make do with reusable cloths.

Hanging up the washing in the dimly lit bathroom, it attracted the moths.

We failed in our duty when one day Pete came into painful harm.

Hot water spilled over him to scald his stomach and arm.

So now there were six to fit into a single bedroom.

And when grandma visited she slept in the living room.

The black-and-white television only showed BBC.

We didn't even have a radio when there was nothing to see.

Maybe that explains why I had a bad nail-biting habit.

Whippings and threats couldn't stop me nibbling my digits.

Other mental scars included not wanting to be touched.

Even casual contacts were psychologically too much.

There were times when I contemplated running away from home.

But my worst desire was to be an orphan, for no one to come.

Into my dreams I escaped from the harsh mundane reality.

What others consider nightmares, I had a party.

One recurring scene was my battle with a winged demon down a shaft.

I always won, but back into the dark hole I would descend just to be daft.

My nightly journeys into other realms brought a curious talent.

To foresee future visions that were accurately decent.

Once predicted an Alan Hansen goal in a League Cup final.

And a grey missing out on the Grand National pinnacle.

Mum betted on that horse to win and got angry when it did not.

Brother supported my claim that I foretold it coming third on the dot.

That incident got me trying to dream for betting on winning finishers.

And that is why I lost my godly gift, corrupted by desire for easy riches.

At eleven I moved to secondary schooling with a new teaching boss.

From mixed classes to all boys at Hillfoot Hey in Hunts Cross.

On first day a stranger came knocking on our chip shop door.

A fellow new student introduced himself as Adrian Ball.

We walked and talked all the way to our new high school.

He became my first real best friend, who I thought was really cool.

One day Adrian came into my class and got me to play pitch and toss.

Whoever got their coin closest to the wall would profit, and the others registered a loss.

I later incorporated this into a marbles game with coins as targets.

Using my lunch money I pulled in the gambling maggots.

My reputation as a gaming shark was attracting the wrong souls,

For I started hearing abuse on my color and other verbal lows.

It was the first time I faced outright racism.

Made me realize why murderers and idiots like Fascism.

There was one particular fat blond boy that continually spat racist hate.

As an adopted Liverpudlian I gave plenty of foulmouthed rebates.

If I was bigger, I would probably have jumped on his face.

But I was happy when an even nastier kid beat me to that race.

Though I appeared to act badly, my childhood criminality was a letdown.

Hurling snowballs at buses and trespassing on sacred ground.

Caught climbing his tree, the vicar gave me a verbal reprimand.

Had to hunt for horse chestnuts elsewhere to avoid the holy man.

Christmas was the only time I went back to the church legally.

Along with the school choir I sang the festive songs cheerfully.

"Away in a Manger" and "Silent Night" were two of my favorites.

I even recited the Lord's Prayer but not with the passion of zealots.

The truth is, I am morally infested with a good sense of conscience.

Once I took an ice cream bar from a newsagent in sneaky voidance.

None caught my criminal act of shoplifting but me.

Guilty as charged, I returned the stolen good before I fled.

I didn't pry into my family's love affairs, being naïve about the birds and bees.

Even at thirteen I thought sucking a woman's breast would make babies.

First time we met Yin Keong Ngeow was him driving us around in London.

We were packed into his Mini car with barely any seat for me to sit on.

He was graduating from medical school when he dated my sister Kwee.

His father was a prominent physician, brewing a large Malaysian family tree.

Just as I was getting comfortable with an education in gaming and no female,

Family packed up shop and settled in the new town of Skelmersdale.

Trying to recall something nice about the place, but I can't think of anything.

Back to an all-mixed Glenburn High School, but even that was depressing.

Times were so boringly bad for me that I finally took seriously my schooling,

Although the bigger incentive was to avoid a chronic life working in servicing.

I was forced to help out with the family business when class was over.

Most customers are nice, but the few racist morons make you want to take cover.

First day they dumped me into the lowest math class.

Teacher elucidating fractions as a frustrating task.

Turned to test me for which I easily answered.

Told him I did more advanced arithmetic as normal manner.

Before the lesson was finished I was moved to a higher division.

I focused on improving my studies from there on with no diversion.

For my core curriculum subjects I picked mainly science courses.

English was mandatory, otherwise I would have shot it like a lame horse.

Literature and language were two separate classes to double my humiliation.

Reading Thomas Hardy's *Mayor of Casterbridge*, I renamed it *Major Castration*.

In hindsight, the punishment was a true blessing in disguise.

Otherwise my attempts to write these verses would be a total demise.

Next time I recalled seeing Keong with my sister was at their wedding banquet.

I knew no one at the large gathering except for my family and the marrying duet.

The large Ngeow clan was drinking and eating their fill.

Made my parents hide when it came to paying the bill.

We had a small private celebration at our store for the newlyweds.

My dad carved exquisite vegetable decorations from which we fed.

A true professional, he spent all night perfecting his curry puffs.

He cried each time the pastry did not rise with the right stuff.

The perfection and generosity I got from my father's gene.

My mother gave me the boldness to be competitively keen.

Our Singaporean relatives would visit us rarely.

But Grandma would come almost yearly.

My mum told me I was her favorite grandson,

Yet her presence brought me no fun.

The day she passed away I was told she was waiting for me.

No tears till I saw her in a casket and knew she would no longer be.

This would not be the only time I was cold to the living.

Only in death would a burning hell be stoked up in my feelings.

Playground gambling days were past me, replaced by legit activities.

In tag games I escaped my pursuers by hurdling high fences with ease.

But my newfound love affair was with football.

Playing with anything that I could kick against a wall.

I even competed in a match on a swollen ankle that I couldn't fit back into my shoe.

The Reds of Liverpool is my favorite local club and not Everton, the team in blue.

Bill Shankly, a Scot, was worshipped by the red half of Merseyside.

Manager of Liverpool Football Club, he put together the best British side.

Keegan and Toshack were the "little and large" who terrorized oppositions.

Emlyn Hughes, nicknamed Crazy Horse, captained the team to win many competitions.

Three League titles, two FA Cups, and a UEFA Cup before retiring.

Shankly was renowned for his witty quotes that were all inspiring.

Fans standing on the Kop chant his name and sing the club's anthem.

"You'll Never Walk Alone" filled the Anfield ground in celebrating triumph.

Isaac Newton ruled classical physics with his fundamental laws of mechanical motion.

Calculus, he developed to explain a falling apple, would start a mathematical revolution.

History has marked him down as perhaps the greatest and most influential scientist.

Philosophiae Naturalis Principia Mathematica, published in 1687, is on the all-time master list.

To learn the foundation of science is to follow Newton's historical discoveries.

His theories can explain the kicking of a football to the rotation of galaxies.

Chemistry and physics were my best subjects in which I saw a practical future.

The way it was taught bored me with math for its abstract nature.

I also enjoyed history, covering the violence of the Greek and Roman Empires.

When it turned into the British Industrial Revolution, I became less inspired.

O-Level exams produced only As in Mathematics and Physics.

But my most satisfying passing grade was a C in my dreaded
English.

It was time to graduate up to Skelmersdale Sixth Form College
to study A-Levels.

Chose chemistry, mathematics, and physics to continue my
studies and avoid stupid evils.

Although we learned the basics of the quantum world,
Newtonian mechanics was still king.

Everyday observables, we could use his three laws of motion to
accurately pin.

And with differential and integral calculus you can determine
the changing world.

I saw through science the answers to everything and all things
spiritual to be curtailed.

The bureaucrats decided to turn Skelmersdale into a New Town
development.

Located twenty kilometers northeast of Liverpool, it brought in
the local migrants.

Our chippy was in the older part of town, known locally as Old
Skem.

With nothing of cultural interest, it was about as much fun as
playing in a chicken pen.

Near to my college was the Concourse Shopping Centre.

The only highlight moments were mindless browsing when I
would enter.

Perhaps fate has intended to put me into such a depressing situation.

So I was motivated to pursue higher learning to escape my depression.

I'd a tough call deciding whether chemistry or physics had more of my adoration.

Chemist seems to have fun blowing things up and making smelly concoctions.

Finally settled when my physics teacher boasted he was married to a beautiful wife.

Using naïve logic, I concluded women prefer physicists to be part of their life.

Experiences have taught me that being handsome and rich are the real priorities.

And that ugly, poor nerds exaggerate how sexy are their partners' extremities.

But I guess using sex for a chosen destiny is as good as tossing a coin.

Head or tail cannot compete with fantasizing on curvaceous loins.

So whether the reasons were stupid or it was just fate, I traveled down the science path.

Except for one coming incident, I never again foretold the future and provoked God's wrath.

There was also a separation in my developing interest in advanced math.

Measurements and experimental observations I considered being the real task.

After completing a year in advanced studies, it was time to ponder universities.

I considered myself too dumb for Cambridge or Oxford, the greatest of academic cities.

My main criterion was to be near my favorite football club.

So first name on the selection form was Liverpool, my real true love.

Lancaster, Salford, Leeds, and Manchester were listed as optional,

Although the Uniteds of Leeds and Manchester were my bitter soccer rivals.

The grade requirement for entering Liverpool University was three Cs.

As backup, I selected Lancaster, who offered entry needing only two Es.

Even though I'd confidence in passing my A-Level exams,

It was still a nervous result day at the college camp.

An A in chemistry, but surprisingly only Bs in physics and mathematics,

Considering I comfortably finished the tests early without having to be frantic.

But the unrest was short-lived, knowing I was to continue my higher education.

Finally I could escape my parents' dreadful life of toil and stagnation.

Wigan and Ormskirk were nearby towns where I took my driving instructions.

Failed my driver's tests so many times for frivolous infractions.

For not glancing into the rear mirror or missing the signal indicator.

People joked that I should wear a skirt and bed the instructors.

Dad allowed me to drive his brown Datsun while registering for test dates.

Until finally I passed and could joyfully take down the L learner's plates.

I continued to live at home even though I was now a big boy at university.

The physics department was up Brownlow Hill in the heart of the city.

My dad used the car before dawn to pick up fresh supplies from the markets.

The rest of the time I drove to classes like an idiot for road-rage targets.

If there is one lesson I should definitely take, it's anger management.

Not surprising that teenage boys pumped with testosterone have highest insurance payments.

Free board and delicious meals were advantages to home living.

But it sucks when it comes to dating and socializing.

First year I made no friends with teachers or students.

It wasn't until David Thornley snuck up to me like a quiet rodent.

Not sure if he felt sorry for me or was after my bag of sweets.

Found out he was a Reds football fanatic, which made it a real treat.

He also lived with his parents in Childwall district.

Close to our former Gateacre home where my upbringing was strict.

So we had much in common, including having no girlfriends.

In physics there were a few girls, but most looked more like men.

Now that I was in higher education I was exempt from the family business.

I stayed upstairs copying that day's scribbled lectures into neat pamphlets.

Memorizing notes is, in my opinion, not the best learning method.

You pass exams, but understanding the subject needs more studious effort.

We rarely got work assignments, and it was almost impossible to get termination.

So there was no motivation to study hard until the end-of-year examinations.

The only course that had a weekly assessment was laboratory experiments.

From measuring the finite speed of light to determining charged particle movements.

Random and systematic errors are an experimentalist's true judge.

You can make any results fit if you're willing to fudge.

Other than by dishonesty, there is no hiding from the error bars.

These experimental uncertainties will let others know whether you're on par.

Non-scientists tend to perceive whatever they hear and see as absolute.

They ought to be taught that even in science there are achievable flukes.

From the absolute domain of Newton came Albert Einstein's relative world.

For observers traveling close to the speed of light, Newtonian principles begin to fail.

There are no privileged reference frames, and the universe is policed by a maximum speed limit.

Length contraction and time dilation are a consequence of approaching the velocity summit.

This is the law of special relativity proposed in 1905 by the patent clerk.

Paradoxical, the greatest genius of our century was rejected for a teaching berth.

General Relativity was published in 1916 and incorporated gravity into his relativistic framework.

Curvature of unified space-time can lead to black holes where even photons are gravitationally cork.

Einstein is best remembered for his equivalence relationship between energy and mass.

$E=mc^2$ is the most recognizable scientific equation that led to the nuclear bomb blast.

Less known is his Nobel Prize in 1921 for his description of the photoelectric effect,

An experiment supporting quantum mechanics' description of the atomic world that was perfect.

Yet the uncertainty of the quantum realm cannot reconcile with Einstein's theories of the cosmos.

"God does not play dice," was his rebuke to quantum indeterminism, which he considered hogwash.

I was not a good brother to Pete; used to dangle him over the balcony.

Perhaps I was jealous he was dad's favorite son, which festered disharmony.

The only benefit I gave him was the motivation to go one better than me.

Always reminds me that he has one higher level master degree.

Another advantage with having a brutish brother was he never feared bullies.

If he could survive my tantrums, then the rest of society appeared like girlies.

Sister Kwee had moved to America with her husband.

She visited us often with her new daughters in hand.

Swee May was my first niece, a royal pain to babysit.

Demanded bottles of milk each night or else she threw a fit.

Swee Ping was the opposite with her baby temperament.

I could dump her in the corner by herself with contentment.

There was a scary moment one night when May tumbled down the stairs.

Luckily with all that padded milky fat she survived, none the worse for wear.

I had no idea what I wanted to do after graduation.

A meandering soul lacking purpose and motivation.

W ithout real conviction I strolled to the head of department.

Offer of a graduate program in nuclear physics was accepted with wonderment.

Forever I am indebted to the British taxpayers for free education.

And political supporter of a democratic socialist state operation.

The national health offered free medical to all citizens.

Strong mind and body will work to return the benefits to fellow denizens.

L abour was the political party of the socialist lefties.

Confronted from the right by the conservative Tories.

Liberal was a fringe party in a two-horse Parliamentary race.

Of no democracy stood the House of Lords an unelected place.

Queen Elizabeth was the symbolic head upon her coronation.

Legacy of former colonial conquests was the Commonwealth League of Nations.

Singapore joined the Commonwealth in 1966 to become one with many.

Same year when England won the World Cup against Germany.

There were many trade union strikes and disruptions in the seventies.

Uncollected rubbish and blackouts were common nasties.

It brought down the Labour Party, and in came the Iron Lady.

She beat up on the unions and privatized the national entities.

Unemployment skyrocketed, and in Liverpool a quarter of adults had no jobs.

Collecting dole money and in some cases supplementing income with criminal mobs.

Just as Thatcher seemed doomed to lose her prime minister post

Came the Falklands war with Argentina that gave her a winning toast.

Battle pride revitalized a nation, while the Argies threw out their military dictator.

So the spilling of blood was ultimately political benefit to the losers and victors.

Other than my late grandma, the only Singaporean who visited us regularly was Teck Chuan.

Eldest cousin worked as a mechanic on Singapore Airlines so could fly free when he wanted.

On graduating with a bachelor in science it was my first time to return to my birthplace.

Though I hated the hot weather, the delicious feasting was a most welcome-back taste.

Each day was a happy perpetual routine of eating, showering, and chatting.

Recalling forgotten faces and names of family members I was reacquainting.

My cousin Kwee Eng and her husband took me on a driving tour into Malaysia.

We ended up in Genting, a casino resort that was my first professional gambling fantasia.

Singapore was no longer the place I remembered in time.

It was a grown-up nation that had left me and its poor past behind.

I carried its roots within my soul, but for now I was no longer an Asian.

England was where I would return to continue my life as a Caucasian.

My nuclear research supervisor was Arthur James.

As an undergraduate lecturer he was a royal pain.

But he was highly regarded as a brilliant scientist.

As his first graduate student I was pampered like a royalist.

I was assigned to dumb duties such as Monte Carlo simulations.

Even then Trevor Morrison programmed all the difficult computations.

My doctorate thesis would be on the development of the Recoil Separator,

A mass identifier of heavy ions produced from a Van de Graaff accelerator.

The Nuclear Structure Facility was located at Daresbury in the Cheshire County.

In its time it was one of the world's best nuclear structure research facilities.

For the first time in my life I lived away from home,

Though less than an hour drive if my mum told me to come.

Started off in university dorm a stone's throw from the physics department.

Moved to a basement flat I shared for five pounds a week rent.

Toxteth was a rough neighborhood some considered a slum.

Poor students, drug dealers, muggers, and an assortment of bums.

One of my fellow students and near neighbors would constantly get mugged.

As a psycho with a conscience I went prowling for these low-life bugs.

Closest I came was twice when encountered by gangs of three.

Whatever they saw in my evil eyes made them step back and flee.

My dad brought me my own automobile.

A red Fiat coupe that barely fit four to fill.

Had a wheel stolen and nail jammed into my ignition.

Probably the same muggers I scared off, wanting retribution.

Had to park my car securely at the campus and walk instead.

Most nights the only person strolling down dark lanes to his lonely bed.

There was a pink Rolls Royce with which the neighborhood gang did not mess.

Belonged to the criminal kingpin that even a madman would not test.

The police once raided the local drug den.

Next day a full-blown mass riot as anarchy did ascend.

I casually walked past burning cars and news camera crews.

Had a more important snooker practice match to pursue.

Life for me in academic research was cozy and an easy take.

Went into the department in time for the morning coffee break.

An hour playing cribbage before it was time for lunch.

More cribbage, more breaks, and then some data to crunch.

Cannot blame work-related stress for my nightly mugger hunting.

Scared off girls as easy as criminals, which meant sex was lacking.

Theory of primeval frustration was reinforced by a close friend.

David Burrows was even crazier than I until a girl made him mend.

Once I took a train to visit the loving couple.

We were assaulted at the station by a gang of mindless muscles.

Before he found love, my buddy would have waded in like a maniac.

It was left to me to put aside my pretense to be a peace-loving brainiac.

Dave did try to pull me aside from the mass attack.

For his courage he was whacked with an iron bar from the railway track.

I did take down one fat assailant with a front snap kick to his groin.

Fond memories of his painful squeal as he collapsed on his quivering loin.

The leader of the gang of eight seemed perturbed I would not back down.

Insisting he was a jujitsu master made him look even more of a clown.

Throwing down their weapons and words, they escaped on a coming train.

Police were called to arrest them while I attended to my friend's pain.

Lacking evildoers to vent my simmering anger upon,

I signed up with the university sports club for training to take on.

The instructors were members of the British Ju-Jitsu Association.

Soke Brundell was the founder, with Lowlands as the center of veneration.

My fellow university students were too much soft puss for my liking.

So I followed the masters to where I could get a good hard beating.

The bloodstains on the dojo mats were from those taking their black belts.

Soon I rose in the ranks to know how the masters felt.

Other university sports that I partook were football and cricket.

Renowned for my tough tackling and wild bowling that took few wickets.

Only winning triumph came in an indoor five-a-side interdepartmental tournament.

Provided the assist to Andy Kirwan to score for our winning highlight moment.

Brother Pete was a guest player for one of the other rival teams.

Hit in the eye with the ball detached his retina seam.

As with my usual uncaring manner, I gave no sibling love or sympathy.

Bad karma inflicts upon me future double retinal detachments for my emotional apathy.

Lost my big science virginity the day the Recoil Separator was commissioned.

Surprisingly pleased that my computer simulations came to real-life fruition.

High-energy gamma-ray emissions were measured in coincidence with the ion mass.

From the decay sequence the energy structure of a nucleus could be unmasked.

Spectroscopic discoverer of the super-deformed cerium-124 isotope was my scientific fame.

Though the crowning published research paper was actually written by Paul Nolan in my name.

Theories for my written thesis came from copying other researchers' works.

My contribution to the advancement of science was of little groundbreaking perks.

Not surprising, my first submission was rejected by the assessors.

An anticlimax when I was finally passed by the professors.

But at least now I could put doctor to the front of my official title.

And most rewarding was the pride to my family's credentials.

My father suffered a stroke, which incapacitated him.

The callous son that I was gave no feelings to what was grim.

As with my grandma, I will forever walk a lonely path seeking forgiveness.

Yet this may be my godly destiny to wander my own inner wilderness.

My torment is ease, knowing my father was proud of my achievements.

Mother told me he boasted around his friends of my academic accomplishments.

Father's younger brother came from Shanghai to stay with our grieving family.

Uncle would be a valuable asset to my own business startup calamity.

I invented the Strika, an impact force and timing instrument.

Used by training martial artists for punching and kicking measurement.

My uncle's tailoring experience was used to stitch the padded implements.

Business partner Phil Bishop built the electronic components.

Marketing and sales were my main responsibility.

Soon realized for real commerce I had infant naïveté.

Humbled by my failure in entrepreneurship due to my lack of business acumen,

I broke off the partnership and stashed my invention aside for the moment.

Applied for regular nine-to-five jobs in areas of advanced technologies.

Went for appointment in London with a company in the cryogenic industries.

Interviewed by Jim Hutchins and Peter Jarvis for position of project engineer.

Imagining them to be my fighting opponents, I won myself a new career.

Our family had a semi-detached house in the mega metropolis of London.

Located in Cricklewood just north of the large Irish community of Kilburn.

Drove south in my Fiat to share the home with my cousin Mona Sim.

She was the daughter of my eldest aunty Lim.

Her desires were an Italian boyfriend and gardening.

Bitched whenever I kicked a ball into her plantings.

Started daily driving the seven miles to my office in the London district of Acton.

But after a harrowing two-hour experience stuck in traffic, to the bus I took on.

Cryogenic Consultants was located in an old warehouse building.

Shared a ground floor office with my boss Jim as I was learning.

Designing low-temperature systems and superconducting magnets.

Worked long hours, including weekends, to quickly become an expert.

Martin Chappell was a technician earning extra money cutting hair at lunchtime.

As his colleague and customer, he soon became a best friend of mine.

He took me to his local gym where we worked out and combat sparred.

Kicked me in the eye, but at least he drove me to the hospital in my car.

After the operation I had to rest two weeks for my recuperation to end.

First day home I did a backward somersault for a visiting friend.

Not surprising, the surgery did not succeed, which almost made me cry.

Finally decided to take surgeon's advice when he went back into my eye.

Once healed to live a peaceful life, the doctors recommended, was impossible.

Went back sparring with Martin, and this time his turn to end up in hospital.

An unblocked punch to his eye gave him a bloody hemorrhage.

Forever our lasting friendship is bonded through a violent heritage.

He moved in to share the house with me and Mona.

But soon he emigrated to be with his parents in America.

After the passing of Dad, my mother and sister remained in Southport.

Business was poor when they transitioned to a Chinese restaurant they bought.

Peter was now at a university in Manchester studying as a chemical engineer.

He would help out in the family business whenever at home he appeared.

Grand opening I also showed up to help, but threatened to punch a customer.

It perplexes me why racist idiots make stupid remarks to a food server.

The restaurant was quickly sold, and my mother finally retired.

Cher went to work as a waitress for a friend's restaurant empire.

In her retirement, mum would come and look after me in London.

Martin quickly became my mother's favorite adopted son.

Not used to a lazy life, she would work feverishly around the house.

From building a garden fence to blocking up holes to keep out field mice.

When Martin left the country, he still took his family to visit my mum up north.

He set a loving example for me, which I seemed incapable of being taught.

One day I was sent to pick up a customer arriving at the airport from Australia.

As I returned to the company, I was told to send him away due to internal mania.

Our company was declared bankrupt, and the bank's appointed receiver was now in charge.

Absurdly business was booming, but management did not pay attention to the cash flow chart.

As fate would have it, I was offered another job a week before this catastrophic event.

So it was an easy decision to pack up, and to the new company I went.

Magnex Scientific was based in Abingdon, an hour drive west.

For the first month I commuted by car, which wasn't the best.

I then decided to stay at bed and breakfast places during midweek.

Driving back to London Friday night, following this routine for several weeks.

David Rayner was the opposite general manager to Jeremy Good.

My former employer was technologically smart under his hood.

But the new one was only interested in running corporate affairs.

Though he still had energy to bed the secretary in a love affair.

Fed up with the long weekly commute, I took up an offer from Ian Jenkins.

Another graduate from Liverpool, so a readymade reference to get me in.

The Kilns was a historical home of C. S. Lewis, which was now a rundown mess.

My bedroom was the attic, where supposedly the famous wardrobe was kept.

We shared the large house with a young couple and a medicated schizophrenic.

The madman threatened to kill the other tenants until he met a crazier maniac.

Maybe it's because I also walk along a narrow edge of insanity.

Fearing my violent temperament meant he still had some sense of reality.

The director Richard Attenborough viewed our place as a potential movie setting.

Decided to build a replica of the house at Pinewood Studios for the filming.

Shadowlands was on the life of Lewis, an Oxford professor,

Though he is more world-renowned as a fantasy author.

A friend of Tolkien, he was once a skeptic of all things spiritual.

We traveled along parallel journeys in finding the godly virtues.

We were all kicked out of the Kilns after the madman reported our slum landlord to the police.

Trustees wanted no bad publicity on Lewis's legacy so terminated our renter's lease.

I moved to a new house, sharing with my old boss Jim and friend Richard Tanner.

Rick hid from fellow Liverpool alumni and family his gay manner.

Before long his Indian lover Siddo moved in with us.

Jim, a traditional married man, luckily didn't put up any fuss.

After the bankruptcy he got an offer in Oxford through his job search.

Like me, before he had commuted home at the end of each work week.

Downtown Los Angeles was start of my tour when I visited Martin in California.

Policemen pointing guns at suspects is not the best welcome sight to America.

Still, as a dumb, excited tourist, I wanted my photo taken at the crime scene.

My friend hastily pulled me away from the urine-smelling street that was mean.

Work also sent me across the pond as a service engineer.

Visited more peaceful scenic places working with my peers.

From the sunny beaches of Santa Barbara to the snowy peaks of Colorado.

I decided the United States of America was where I wanted to go.

My company told me they would satisfy my desire and post me abroad.

After a year with no permanent work visa I was starting to get bored.

Drunk at a barbecue party, I finally broke down and wept in front of my friend.

The following day I handed in my resignation letter for my employment to end.

Instead they tempted me with higher promotion and more money.

Being a weak soul I accepted the bribe even though I knew it to be temporary.

On a foreign assignment I got forwarded a job description.

Even before I returned home I sent off my application.

Things move quickly when you are a wanted man.

Out west to a desert town in Arizona and not just for a tan.

My new boss was to be Eric Swartz, the owner's son.

Working at Research and Manufacturing Company located in Tucson.

HEADING WEST TO PHANTOM RICHES

(1993-2002)

The pioneers in sailing vessels built a towering nation.

It took wings of death to rain down tears of passion.

Exploring a new chapter of my life upon a third continent.

Like pilgrims, before I carried in my bag dreamy sentiments.

In reality, life never unfolds like a Disney's fairy-tale fantasy.

Moments when it's more like a horror show tragedy.

Maybe not the land of the brave and free of the founding fathers.

But here at last I felt at home with a calling that will honor my mother.

Had to find myself a new apartment and a new car in a new land.

Needed a US license; otherwise getting an auto was banned.

Glumly trudged my way into the driver center to book a test.

Expecting, like England, to wait weeks, which would put me in a mess.

When asked to pick my own appointment date, I sarcastically stated immediately.

Was astounded when requested payment to start the test promptly.

This was my first gratifying immersion in the capitalist life of an American.

With a positive new attitude that money can buy you anything, I was an instant fan.

The nightmares of my past failed tests came back to haunt me.

Making me more nervous was driving the opposite side to what it used to be.

Examiner noted I went off the road and didn't halt at a stop junction.

The most shocking experience was actually getting a pass certification.

Tucson had possibly the worst combination of highway commuters.

Lax testing to allow control of fast-moving metal machines to beginners.

Alien smugglers from the nearby border driving in banged-up vehicles.

Retirees coming for their winter retreats, known as snowbirds to the locals.

And young University of Arizona students that drove like clowns.

Not surprising road accidents were a common sight in this western town.

I picked myself an old ugly yellow clunker of a car from an even shabbier dealer.

Two thousand dollars for a Subaru station wagon that drove like a tanker.

At least I wasn't afraid to play bumper cars with the rest of the lousy drivers.

In cowboy country the real danger was the road-rage pistol-packing gunners.

Back then gasoline was a dollar a gallon.

Cheaper than bottled water from the fountain.

Periodically the gears disengaged and transmission was disabled.

Had to go under the hood to hand tighten the clutch cable.

Kept contemplating to take my junk to a scrap dealer's pound.

But like an aging companion dog, I didn't have the heart to put it down.

Was told to avoid apartments to the west due to the early morning sun.

Driving into the full glare of our bright star was definitely no fun.

South are the civilian and military airports and little else but nature.

Mountain ridges of the Catalina Foothills mark the northern border.

So I picked a rental furnished place to the east side of downtown.

With home and ride settled, I could finally focus on my work now.

The Swartzes had brought me on board to teach them the secrets of superconductivity.

Eric had a brilliant mind but ran his father's company incompetently.

Taught him to build a magnet the traditional method with an aluminum mandrel.

But was overridden and told to save costs and used glued-on plastic handles.

When the high-field superconducting magnet blew up on energizing,

The damaged good was dumped on my table for a miracle fixing.

Although research and manufacturing were in their corporate name,

They seemed to treat it more as an inventor's club for seeking fame.

It didn't take me long to realize I'd gotten myself in with bad employers.

Not just because of my personal opinion but the dubious financial numbers.

Worse, I discovered them telling the community it was because of my failure.

Years later Eric had the decency to apologize for treating my reputation like manure.

I was surprised by his admission and seeking for forgiveness.

Turned out he was dying of cancer and wanted solace from tarnished business.

My American sister had applied for immigration rights for our entire family.

It took only a couple of years for our mother to get her legal entry.

Siblings had lower priority and processing would take many more years.

Too long for me to wait since the stability of my job I feared.

I was on an employment visa that tied me in with the company.

And my corporate boss refused to sponsor for my permanent residency.

Exercise is a good channel to vent work-related stress.

So I took up sporting activities in the midst of my status mess.

Soccer and kung-fu was where I tried out my physical might.

Instead of my colleagues I used competitors to fight.

The indoor soccer arena was my first experience of a coed tournament.

In one game I grabbed an inappropriate body part on a female opponent.

Luckily she took no offense and even smiled at my attacking action.

I had to readjust my gentleman's game for the ladies in motion.

I formed my own team from my fellow workers.

Even got Eric and his wife to become players.

When an ex-marine showed photos of kittens savaged by his pit bulls.

It was left to me to throw him off our company's team for being so cruel.

He wasn't fired from his job as a psychological sicko.

Carrying a .45 Magnum into work perhaps deflated his scared boss's gusto.

In martial arts there is no hiding place for cowards.

A true warrior always fights moving forward.

Sifu Fong was the Wing Chun master I followed under the western sun.

He was trained alongside Bruce Lee by grandmaster Yip Man.

I found the soft flowing forms to be difficult in practicing.

Counter to the hard style of jujitsu I'd so many years in training.

Bruce Lee said one should master all styles to be a great fighter.

So, taking my hero's advice, I also studied tae kwon do, kickboxing, and others.

My mother would stay several months with me in Tucson,

Sharing parental time with Cher in England and Pete in Hong Kong.

Regularly took her to flea markets to hunt for bargains.

Even a twenty-five-cent cup she would barter for lower price gains.

Money had no value to me other than how fast I could spend it.

Each paycheck I would at least load my mum with a fair bit.

I introduced her to my colleague Yi-Hua Tang and his family.

She also became close with Mei Kuenhold, whom she met in a grocery.

Martin lived in the adjacent state of California.

Five hundred miles apart, which Americans consider near.

In England a fifty-miles drive is a major excursion.

There is such a huge mental difference in perceptions.

It is the reverse when historical times are referenced.

Yankee history extending beyond a century is ancient.

Europeans talk about centuries as if it were yesterday.

And for Asians, only millenniums are considered a long way.

Andrew Kirwan was the first visiting friend from back home.

Visitors' tours included the cowboy town of Tombstone.

Cross the Mexican border south into Nogales.

A place that was dull and featureless.

When Dave and Mary Morrison visited, we had much more fun.

Ended up in Las Vegas, the gambling city in the desert sun.

Life in America was not all about playing and partying.

Working to pay the bills with a bad company was depressing.

Applied for a residence permit to allow me to move freely.

Had to pay the immigration attorney with my own money.

Went down the riskier channel as an outstanding researcher.

A more fast-track way to get my green card than as a regular worker.

Filled in the application forms and even the company's sponsored letter.

Had Dave Swartz sign the paperwork when his mood was better.

Almost ended up joining the US military.

Browsing the recruitment centers I was invited in by the navy.

Curiosity got the better of me and I took the tests for cadet evaluating.

Passed with flying colors and told to get ready for boot camp training.

They couldn't find a pay scale for a graduate with a doctorate degree.

Naval HQ also confirmed never encountering such a high academic entry.

I would have joined if they granted me immediate citizenship.

Was told as a foreigner I would not be allowed to serve on nuclear ships.

Comical scenario of a nuclear physicist sweeping decks on a destroyer.

And the fact I'm prone to seasickness, I decided sensibly to decline their offer.

Company was starting to lay off workers and I sensed my turn was coming.

Even though I was a salaried employee, my wage checks were fluctuating.

To stay in the country, my application had to come through now or never.

What was supposed to take three months seemed to drag on forever.

Half a year from submission I finally got called in for an interview.

On the day my attorney was nervous, but I was of stronger will.

My session was videotaped by the immigration officer at the interrogation helm.

A few minutes of my technological bullshit and he was already overwhelmed.

The day I got my first pink slip, Eric was acting very nicely as a boss.

Pulled me to one side to tell me what a talented, hardworking guy I was.

Even though I had prepared myself, it was still bitter to hear I was fired.

But I was professional enough to respond with my own fake words to inspire.

A mother's love and support at such low times is immeasurable,

Especially when she backs the emotional comfort by placing money on the table.

She had saved thousands that I had given her from my wages.

Though it collected no interest, it was far more than what I deposited with the bankers.

Same week I became unemployed, a most welcomed package came in the mail.

My permanent residence was finally approved and I no longer felt I had failed.

This was perhaps the first time that I sensed being spiritually blessed.

Looked after by a guardian angel at moments when my life was in a mess.

Pleasant events were happening, so looking for a new job was not of urgency.

I took up acting classes in front of the camera with Fosi's Talent Agency.

My big moment came with an audition call for a *Star Trek* movie.

I'd Martin send overnight an old pair of his contact lenses so I could look groovy.

Got the role of a Federation engineer onboard the spaceship.

Spent three days filming with the fictitious characters that I worship.

Most memorable incidence was not in front of the camera.

Flicking switches too quickly got me a slap from the director.

Off the set Jonathan Frakes privately apologize for his whack.

I would have been happy even if he'd hit me with a bat.

The premier of my Trekkie motion picture film *First Contact* was 1996.

Made a worldwide announcement of my own to friends and relatives.

My brother's pals in Hong Kong spotted me in the film when it did matter.

Could have been family resemblance or that I was the only Chinese actor.

On the shooting sets they'd jokingly teased me as the grandson of Sulu.

The Asian pilot for Captain Kirk's first generation Enterprise that he flew.

Following a Wing Chun class, I met a local Tucsonian named Matt.

Demonstrated in the backyard his sword fighting skills with a wooden bat.

Hired me to join his company, he started with his friends David, Rich, and Andy.

Rising Technologies produced a Spanish-to-English language
software CD.

It was my first position dedicated purely to marketing and sales,

Though I learned more about playing darts than commercial deals.

One day a stranger called to be let into our office aisle.

Interrupted my practice session aiming for the bullseye.

Interrogated me with many searching questions.

Identified himself as an agent of the FBI after the session.

Apparently an informant had accused me of being a Chinese spy.

Maybe it was my bad dart skills that convinced him the story
was a lie.

I'd rented a room in the house of my colleague David Dent.

Shared with two Dalmatians that followed him wherever he
went.

Development on the software product was going slow.

Not surprising when the financial budget was so low.

The main investors were Matt's separated parents.

Board meetings were argumentative and an irritant.

This time it was dart and wrestling to vent my physical aggression.

I grappled with David and Andy for bragging rights domination.

Rich was the artistic soul with the finesse on the dart board.

Cricket was my favorite game where I would try to point hoard.

To supplement my income I consulted for a local entrepreneur named John Hess.

A holocaust survivor from a tragic history when humanity was a satanic pest.

He tinkered with cryocoolers to operate at low cryogenic temperatures.

I designed for him susceptibility coils to determine magnetic structures.

My finances were running lower than my morale.

Yet I was too inept to seek a way out from my mental corral.

In my darkest moments, the cosmos provided a shining light.

Terry Nixon, a former colleague, knew of my plight.

Like me, he had lost his job and resettled in New Hampshire.

Gave a glowing reference to his new employer who then sought me out to hire.

This was my introduction to George Svenconis, owner of Cryo Industries of America.

It was time for me to move east, in opposite migration to the original pioneers.

My time spent in Tucson was short with moments of bitter and sweet.

But it gave me the opportunity to migrate to the US, which was a real treat.

Except for work, the overall experience was enlightening.

The Hollywood stereotype of Yanks was misleading.

I found my native companions to be surprisingly friendly.

Not the scary, brash, loud-mouthed, opinionated baddies.

The rest of the world seems to hate and mistrust Americans.

Yet, like me, they wanted to come and savor the conditions.

Like all superpowers, it does stoke up fear and jealousy.

Until you face the reality that we are one global family.

On the way eastward I flew into Pennsylvania to stay with my sister.

To drive the rest of the way to New Hampshire I lent their Ford Explorer.

It was night when I reached my final destination in Salem.

Not the infamous witch-hunting town in Massachusetts that hung them.

This was the namesake place across the northern state border.

"Live free or die" was the motto of these independent New Englanders.

First day at work I was introduced by George to his family-run company.

Son George Junior was the design engineer with mum running the deliveries.

His daughter handled the office and payroll administration.

Terry, who got me the job, managed the backroom production.

At first I feared this would be another disastrously operated dynasty.

But I was pleasantly surprised by their cooperative working efficiency.

I was an instant hit with the Svenconis with my hardworking ethics and talent.

Most workdays I would outlast my boss so he could go home to be a good parent.

One night it almost cost me my life as I worked alone industriously.

A policeman entered our opened rear door with drawn pistol, suspecting a burglary.

His gun followed my dark shadow as I moved across his line of sight.

Luckily he shouted instead of shooting; otherwise it could have been a deadly plight.

Had to calm down the emotional officer before I went to get him a soda.

His anxiety came from knowing he was a finger pull away from a bloody disaster.

Dave, Martin, and I went to visit my brother in Hong Kong.

To witness China reclaiming territory that it had lost for so long.

Most of the rich inhabitants had escaped to other former British colonies.

Australia and Canada benefited most from the influx of foreign monies.

The fear of Communistic oppression and social changes did not materialize.

Smart governance was to keep the status quo and let things stabilize.

This was a time when I started to feel proud of my Chinese heritage.

Throughout my teenage years I had no Asian friends my own age.

Known as a banana because I was white inside with yellow skin.

Even took Mandarin lessons to try and chat to my ancestral kin.

But found the tonal language very difficult to comprehend.

Ma can be pronounced to mean mother, horse, scold, or hemp.

And the written vocabulary is even more bewildering.

There are thousands of characters that need memorizing.

At least I am fortunate to be eloquent in a language that is most diverse.

English is the universal tongue used predominantly in science and commerce.

Joined dart and pool teams at my local bar in Derry.

Slept on the floor in a studio waiting for a larger unit vacancy.

What was supposed to be temporary turned into two-year occupancy.

Rent was cheap so I put up without the comfort and niceties.

When mother was not visiting and feeding me, I would eat out.

Nearby Chinese place was where I got most of my takeout.

We became close family friends with the Lius, who operated the eatery.

They commuted daily across the state line from south of Boston in Quincy.

New England territories have many ski resorts for active fun in the cold.

Out west in the high Rockies you plow through feet of powdered snow.

On the east coast it's inches of manmade crystals that you have to skate over.

Occasionally Canadian arctic storms would blanket the region in white cover.

Took Martin and my brother to a ski vacation in the Italian Alps.

First lesson for Pete was pushing him off the summit without help.

My training philosophy in life is one based on swim or drown.

Only the brave and dedicated prosper and none of the weaker clowns.

Thirteenth October 1998 was a landmark date.

The day at the Argonne National Laboratory that transformed my fate.

Began writing a novel as I sat through a quiet exhibition.

Leo and the Wolfcat emerged from this fantasy science fiction.

KLYSTAR would be the ultimate culmination of this published epic.

A journey of discovery with godly ramification that is truly cosmic.

A rival company, Janis, came headhunting for my skills.

Leaving for George's former employer would have been a bitter pill.

So he was eager to increase my pay when I told him of the approach.

But it didn't keep the hunting recruiters from trying to poach.

Finally I succumbed to the tempting lures dangled in front of me.

Agreed to join Everson Electric located in the Lehigh Valley.

Unlike the last two career moves, this was a relatively short ride.

From New Hampshire to Pennsylvania was a four-hour drive.

Packed my worldly possessions into the motor.

What I couldn't take went into the dumpster.

Bethlehem was my new home and job promotion up the rank.

Namesake to the biblical city on Palestine's West Bank.

Vice president was my fancy new title to go with the higher salary.

As with all imaginary ego trips, it quickly deflates with incoming reality.

In charge was David Everson, who took over a third-generation business.

This was to be another collapsing corporate empire that I was to witness.

Building and repairing locomotive engines was the company's main targets.

Progress to winding and impregnating coils for resistive magnets.

They wanted to tap my expertise in cryogenics and superconductors.

Turn a heavy industry into a precision instrument manufacturer.

Achieve this goal with a patented cryogen-free superconducting invention.

Additional duties included setting up a network for international distribution.

Adam Stadtmuller returned to influence my life that would be dynamic.

A former colleague during my first employment at Cryogenics.

The fact our paths reunite at this critical juncture is truly eerie.

After our corporate demise, he got a new job headquartered in Erie.

Eriez and Everson were already established business partners.

So both our new employers would once more bring us together.

Eriez contacted Everson for their next-generation magnetic separators.

Knowing of my technical experience, they wanted us to be their maker.

Adam visited our facility and we talked professionally on the design.

The world's largest bore cryogen-free superconducting magnet at that time.

To increase the complexity, the coil needed to be wound from niobium-tin wire.

An expensive and brittle material that needed processing in a high-temperature fire.

With Adam's cooperation I came up with a revolutionary new concept.

Based around my patented invention but with even more innovative aspects.

Titanium was selected as the mandrel to wind on the superconductor.

The finished coil's large size made it difficult to load into the furnace reactor.

Disastrous warping happened as we increased the high temperature.

We managed to salvage a coil, but it operated with lower magnetic signature.

Though the collaborative business project was not a total success.

Adam and I became good friends again, so the reunion was not a complete mess.

And his biggest impact on my life achievement was set into motion.

For now we once more went our separate ways, unaware of our final connection.

The script of my sci-fi novel was aimlessly meandering.

I decided to kill off the story in an apocalyptic ending.

It was midnight and a thunderous storm was brewing.

So focused was I on the termination that I ignored the lightning.

To describe Armageddon I needed to put a scene of hell on my laptop.

But four different hellish depictions that I wanted to upload would not.

Two normal astronomical photos popped up without interference.

It was then I knew the universe refused my death sentence.

The morning after I emailed the nightly incident to all my contacts.

Most would have considered my sanity was no longer intact.

But my spirit was as bright as the clear morning sky.

Knowing the heavens would not allow my creation to die.

Neighbor across the hallway was an elderly lady.

Told me of her famous Hollywood son who I thought was a maybe.

Turned out he really did exist when she became gravely ill.

Tod Volpe showed up to sort out her mother's testament and will.

I was the last to see her in the hospice the night she passed.

Following day a shadowy presence visited for a final task.

Her son had fallen on hard times after imprisonment.

From his rich and famous clients he was accused of embezzlement.

I tried to help by buying his artworks and hiring him as a writer.

There were times I felt my generosity was being tested as a giver.

Financial crisis brought down another family-operated dynasty.

Everson was sold off to Tesla Engineering as a subsidiary.

Three colleagues started up their own business ventures.

Following their examples, I headed into an uncertain future.

Ricor in collaboration with Bar Ilan University was my first important client.

Spent a week on their En Harod Ihud kibbutz as a technical consultant.

The community farmed and fabricated stainless steel kitchen ware.

A business offshoot was miniature coolers they fabricated with great precision care.

They wanted the know how to build high-temperature super-conducting magnets.

I developed a unique pancake-stacking coils design that they wanted to patent.

Second consulting client came from a recruiting agency
Aerotek.

Joined Edax as it was transforming to a buyout by Ametek.

What was supposed to be temporary turned into full-time
employment.

Also found myself a new apartment share in Brooklyn Heights
settlement.

Long daily commute to work between New Jersey and New
York.

Spent quarter of an entire day on trains shuttling back and forth.

Nine-eleven will forever be scorched into America's history.

When a band of fanatical terrorists rained down human
butchery.

I was taking a shower when I heard my sister's maid screaming.

We all considered it an accident on seeing the first skyscraper
smoking.

The truth dawned when the plane flew into the second World
Trade Center Tower.

News on the Pentagon strike and air crash further impact on
this disaster.

Roommate Louisa escaped the mayhem across Brooklyn Bridge.

But not for many thousands who perished of innocence and courage.

Recrimination and discrimination spread throughout America.

Worst was to come with wars driven by vengeance and phobia.

GOD POINTS TO
TWIN UNIVERSES

(2002-2007)

They said the second law of entropy could not be conserved.

Yet our single universe defies the first law of energy reserves.

Big Bang marked the chaotic birth of our spirited creation.

Twin universes the orderly expansion of our cosmic evolution.

The truths have been known to many ancient civilizations.

Each advancing culture uses their own natural interpretations.

In Greek myths it started with chaos—an endless dark, silent haven.

Springing forth Gaea, the Mother Earth, and Uranus, the Father Heaven.

In Chinese philosophy Yin and Yang represent dark and light.

Balance for harmonious peace, but as opposing forces they will fight.

Natural order of the universe obeys the law of these twins.

Root of life and death cycle and foundation of all things.

Just before Christmas I was kicked out of the Brooklyn apartment.

A friend accommodated me temporarily in her Astoria residence.

Hunted for stable lodging across the Hudson River in New Jersey.

Decided upon Hoboken for more convenient direct train to work daily.

Tara Greubel was to be my new roommate on First Street.

Across from the Quiet Woman Pub where friends could meet.

Hoboken is a square-mile town bordered by Manhattan-connected tunnels.

Downtown is where traffic through the Holland Tunnel is channeled.

Lincoln Tunnel connects to Midtown near Times Square.

Trains, ferries, and buses offer convenient public transportation fares.

Though I could drive to work, most of the time I took the train.

An hour on the rails compared to traffic-laden roads was less pain.

Used the travel time efficiently working on my laptop.

Some days I barely typed a good sentence before my stop.

Writing is a creative mind game.

When you're in a flow it seems so easily tame.

But a mental block can halt you suddenly in your tracks.

And the harder you try to force it, the more talents you lack.

It can take more than a year to get over the psychological hump.

No rhyme or reasons why you triumph or flump.

At EDAX I was the senior mechanical engineer.

No fancy title but still respected by my peers.

Developed their first cryogen-free X-ray detectors.

By integrating the silicon sensors with Kleemenko cryocoolers.

Company filed a joint patent for another of my novel inventions.

Using thermoelectric coolers and heat pipes for effective conduction.

Pete was accepted into Cornell University graduate business school.

Decided finance was more lucrative profession than the engineering pool.

Got a speeding ticket the first day I drove him to his Ithaca campus.

But his earnings as an investment banker were a more considerable plus.

His internship was at the World Trade Center complex with Lehman Brothers.

When he graduated, the building had been damaged by the terrorist attackers.

Their new Midtown office was located in the heart of the theater district.

The expensive living cost in the nice part of Manhattan was very restrictive.

So I agreed to share the purchase of a Hoboken apartment.

We got a three-bedroom unit with Tara as our live-in tenant.

This was a time when the money lenders were flowing with cash.

Getting a mortgage loan was criminally easier than smoking hash.

For our deposit, Pete used his student loan and I my credit card.

The verification and scrutiny of the bankers was a comical lark.

As least we Ying brothers are responsible professionals.

But many home buyers were naïve or even criminals.

These toxic loans would eventually poison their greedy masters.

Leading to a worldwide economic collapse and social disaster.

Twenty-Second July 2002 marked my second momentous date.

When Adam's spirit would return to influence my chosen fate.

Eureka moment came as the train pulled up at Ho-Ho-Kus Station.

The answer to the ultimate riddle was like a light bulb flashing into ignition.

Rest of the morning, instead of work, I hurriedly scribbled down the formulation.

Universal law of thermodynamics was to be the crowning culmination.

On the last—fourth—page I wrote the conclusion as the proof of GOD.

Determined to garner a Nobel Prize in physics against mighty odds.

In the afternoon I received an incoming international phone call.

The message from a former colleague was a shocking emotional fall.

Miles informed me of the death of our mutual friend, Adam.

His passing soul gave me the cosmic answers I tried so desperately to fathom.

Space is the fabric of energy.

Time is the fabric of entropy.

Energy is the static capacity to work.

Entropy is the dynamic process to work.

There are multiple degrees of energy.

There is a single degree of entropy.

There are multiple space dimensions.

There is a single time dimension.

Energy has dual polarities.

Entropy has dual polarities.

Space points in positive and negative directions.

Time points in positive and negative directions.

Increasing positive energy curves space inward.

Increasing positive entropy moves time forward.

Decreasing negative energy curves space outward.

Decreasing negative entropy moves time backward.

Matter occupies positive time in positive space.

Antimatter occupies negative time in positive space.

Antimatter occupies positive time in negative space.

Anti-antimatter occupies negative time in negative space.

The godly implications of these twin universes is truly cosmic.

Governed by the universal laws of thermodynamics.

Set forth are five divine postulates,

Ruling principles that our cosmos has articulated.

First postulate is our total universe is composed of parallel anti-symmetric systems.

A positive universe and a negative universe with identical duplicated items.

Both worldly realms occupy a common space-time.

My negative twin experiences a universal expansion same as mine.

Second postulate is energy can flow between both universes.

But the total energy in the total universe must be conserved.

This is a compatible principle with the original first law of thermodynamics.

That energy cannot be made or destroyed, but can be converted.

Third postulate is entropy can flow between both universes.

But the total entropy in the total universe must be conserved.

This differs in principle from the original second law of thermodynamics.

But as an isolated observer on my own side of the universe, it does not invalidate it.

Fourth postulate is gravity dictates the direction of entropy change.

This defines the motion of time and over what range.

In our positive universe, gravity is attractive and time is forced forward.

In the twin negative universe, gravity is repulsive and time forced backward.

Fifth postulate is that life on earth exists only in our positive universe.

My negative twin exists in an opposing dual state so that entropy is conserved.

In particle duality, the opposite of a solid body is a fluid wave.

Waves superimpose upon each other and act as one in how they behave.

I am a positive entity with my own individual self-contained body and conscious nest.

My negative twin is merged with all other twins in a single combined consciousness.

In this vast positive universe I am but an insignificant minor cosmic player.

In the negative universe, GOD—the Single Omnipotent Consciousness—is our leader.

Even though the laws of thermodynamics are the foundation of life and science,

A single universe hypothesis with energy appearing from nothing does not make sense.

In a twin universe, equal positive and negative quantities balance out to be zero.

So a universal law of thermodynamics is the perfect cosmic solution to go.

According to standard scientific models, there should be equal amounts of antimatter.

Yet its existence would cause an almighty annihilation and turn our cosmos into tatter.

A minuscule imbalance in parity created a surplus of positive matter in our world.

Reverse parity in the opposite realm produces negative matter to unfurl.

Dark energy is the pervasive cosmic substance that drives an accelerating universe.

Stellar fusion in the negative universe condenses as photons in repulsive reverse.

This vacuum energy released by negative stars stretches the fabric of space-time.

And since both universes share a common membrane, we experience the same expansion in kind.

Dark matter is needed to account for the rapid rotational velocities of galaxies.

Otherwise stars would be flung into outer space, which would give real anxieties.

Repulsive fusion energy stretching intermediate space also compresses the swirling stars.

So a twin universe is most plausible scientific explanation of influence of these dark fluids by far.

Quantum entanglement is when two vastly separated twin particles respond as one.

This phenomenon defies the universal speed limit of light, which it cannot outrun.

Since particle-matters exist as particle-waves in a twin universe domain.

Superposition of twin waves allow for instantaneous interactions to be maintained.

In a one-sided universe with unbalanced baryonic numbers, protons would decay.

If this happened, the very nucleus of our existence would rot away.

Only in a fully balanced cosmos will baryons be conserved.

Once again science has to bow to the reality of dual universes.

We are taught our world exists in four space-time dimensions.

By doubling the universes you should have another four additions.

A common cosmic membrane increases dimensional number by a binary.

Giving a total of ten-dimensions, as with super-symmetric string theory.

All the scientific data points to the true dual nature of our cosmos.

Living such a harmonious balanced existence is a divine kudos.

In science we seek true facts, and in life we seek true love.

Though bound to earth, we can reach out to heaven above.

RISE OF THE DRAGON

(2007-2012)

The fiery beast once hid behind a Great Wall.

With commerce it now soars dominantly over all.

Africa is considered the birthplace of Homo sapiens.

Asia, the cradle of human civilization.

Europe mastered the Industrial Revolution.

America has present-day superpower domination.

But once more China is able to flex its imperious might.

Bolstered by economic expansion and political control that is tight.

With completion of KLYSTAR, it was time to seek out a publisher.

Sent the manuscript to agents and distributors of literature.

Before a vacation to China I decided to call a book publication.

Randomly picked out Tate Publishing, a Christian-based organization.

Spoke to Richard Tate, the founder and chairman of the board.

Found out the previous month we both ran the marathon in New York.

Richard had another common link as an English language teacher in China.

Before returning home to start his own publication house in Oklahoma.

Circulation of my published novel was released in 2007.

When I received the first royalty check it felt like heaven.

I could now add professional author into my curriculum vitae.

Even if there was no hope of retirement from the revenue I was paid.

Not since the Liverpool days did our mother share a home with her two sons.

But the scourge of cancer destroyed the comfort of our reunion.

On her death bed I claimed GOD had promised her continued life.

She could sense my pact was the devil's deceitful strife.

We took our cremated mother's ashes back home to Singapore.

Laid her to rest at Tse Toh Aum Temple with blessings of Buddhist calls.

On the last day of worship a bird fluttered down beside me with gaping beaks.

As I reached out, she flew into the ceremonial offerings to mark a spiritual peak.

Our mother's soul was carried on angelic wings to a godly heaven.

I pray for redemption my fated path will take me to a motherly union.

In our mother's urn we placed soil from our father's English burial site.

Though his remains are in Allerton cemetery, their spirits reunite.

We also visited and burnt blessed offerings to our grandmother Pang Ang.

Her tomb, located at the Singaporean Chinese cemetery of Lim Chu Kang.

My outer physical journey of life has taken me around the globe.

Covering the surface of our planet from head to toe.

My inner spiritual journey of discovery has also come full circle.

From a dream child, bigoted atheist to a preaching vehicle.

Even in my professional occupations the journey was returning to its roots.

Once more a nuclear scientist on Princeton Gamma-Tech Instruments books.

Even the company president was a graduate of Liverpool, where my career begins.

So no matter which direction I headed out, I was fated to return to its origins.

There was a one-year job excursion when I joined Barzel Industries.

A corporation with a radical business philosophy that was revolutionary.

Domenico Lepore was the head wizard at the steering wheel.

Of a heavy industry selling metal alloys and steel.

Decalogue was Domenico's approach to apply scientific logic to commerce.

An incredible methodology that I could relate to and eagerly immerse.

The Conflict Clouds was a powerful tool to tackle problems and develop solutions.

I even applied it to root out the rationale for a godly existence.

Best-laid plans of mice and men can still fall to destruction.

Economic bubble burst in 2009 that brought a global recession.

Lucky for me I was able to go back to work at Princeton.

Pete's bankrupt company, Lehman Brothers, was bought by Barclay's consortium.

Denise Hui was to become my brother's chosen partner.

A beautiful virtue worthy of loving capture.

But nature shows it can be equally cruel as hell.

Infesting her with leukemia to make her unwell.

P ete proposed beside Denise's hospital bed at Memorial Sloan-Kettering.

I was chosen to be my brother's best man at their wedding.

Bone marrow transplant was her only survival path to getting well.

No matching donor was found, so they used umbilical cord stem cells.

Christmas Eve of 2009 was to be a defining moment of discovery.

In the peaceful presence of a recuperating Denise, I solved a major cosmic mystery.

To date, my twin universe concept had no experimental supporting evidence.

Until I developed mathematical calculations that gave my theories proven credence.

By New Year's Eve I had prepared the scientific manuscript for public submission.

Title was "Nuclear Fusion Drives Present-day Accelerated Cosmic Expansion."

In festive mood I registered to present my newfound results at an international conference.

Gathering were experts in cosmology, the quantum vacuum, and zeta functions.

Early in the new year I traveled on business to Saudi Arabia.

There I got the dreaded call from my brother who was in hysteria.

The loving life of Denise was taken away from him.

My journey home was listening to the funeral hymns.

In Bethlehem, the universe had prevented me killing off my KLYSTAR story.

Then came Adam's passing when I got the answers to my twin universe theory.

And culmination to my godly discovery was to be Denise's ultimate testimony.

Until my last breath I fight to win recognition for our sacrifices in a global ceremony.

To respect our mother's memories, we visited her ancestral home in China.

A farming village of Lim on Dongshan Island in the Fujian provincial area.

High-speed trains and skyscrapers reflect the nation's evolving future.

Oxcarts and ancient temples symbolize its historic culture.

On way home we visited our uncle and his family in Shanghai.

A Chinese coastal city with a long history of Western cultural ties.

Along with Beijing and Hong Kong the richest of China's metropolis.

Revisiting father's heritage in nearby Ningbo was added to our to-do list.

I attended my first science workshop motivated by Denise's passing.

Events at the conference would have a major impact that would be lasting.

Held at the Universitat Autònoma de Barcelona over several days.

In celebration of the famed mathematician Emilio Elizalde's sixtieth birthday.

On the first day it snowed in Barcelona, which most of the locals had never experienced.

As in my novel KLYSTAR, the hero character, Leo, is followed by strange weather conditions.

On the last day I was to be the last speaker to present my twin universe proposition.

To my encouraging surprise, it was well received by the intelligent audience with no dissension.

Perhaps the greatest legacy of this Spanish gathering was encountering Ruggero Santilli.

His brilliance on par with Einstein and Newton, the greatest of science majesties.

Fate further took a hand to connect us together.

Testing his invention with our radiation identifier.

Invited by him and his wife Carla to visit them in Florida.

Where I would be a consultant for their enterprising venture.

Wrote, produced, and directed my first theatrical performance.

Based on my poetry of life, love, and remembrance.

Jim Su and Shameely Azanedo were my star performers.

Opening night was at Times Square Art Center.

As part of the visual display, Arnaldo Ugarte crafted the sculptures.

A woman on a crucifix was the controversial centerpiece fixture.

Repeated our performance at the Spur Tree Lounge in the East Village.

Picking a date on the owner Sean John's birthday was like magic.

If the saying is true that there is no rest for the wicked.

Then approaching end of 2010 I was evil incarnated.

Two more science conferences, two weddings, and two historic marathons.

There were two journeys to Greece, the mythical home of the Titans.

Denise's cousin, Carol Ng, united with Wing Cheung in wedded harmony.

My brother Pete acted as the minister for their blessed ceremony.

From the Hong Kong wedding I flew on to Rhodes for a mathematic gathering,

A speaker on my twin universe theories where Ruggero was also presenting.

Ichun Lai and Michael Kitsis was the union of a Chinese and a Jew.

A loving example that transcends any differences in racial or religious pews.

Like my brother and cousin-in-law, the wedded couples met through online dating.

The virtual world of the Internet has become the electronic Cupid for matchmaking.

A commemorative race was to celebrate the Battle of Marathon's 2500-year anniversary

Where the Greeks defeated the Persians and gave birth to democracy.

Along with a group of friends, we followed the original route toward Athens.

Entering the 1896 Olympic stadium was a race finish that could not be beaten.

Not even the luxury to suffer jetlag as I prepared for a home marathon in New York.

Running for Shoe4Africa, which founder Toby Tanser boldly walks more than he talks.

Earn both angelic wings fundraising and making a far-off dream come true

By securing an entry for Eugenia Yuen, so from Australia in she flew.

Our merry charitable band included Tegla Loroupe, a long-distance world champion.

In jest I told her to read a book so she would not bore running with us minions.

Summit of the world was an appropriate end to a momentous year to recall.

In the foothills of the Himalayan Mountains I attended a workshop in Nepal.

Terry Stanley accompanied me at the event coordinated by Kathmandu University.

The prime organizer was Ruggero and his scientific committee.

Third International Conference on Lie-Admissible Treatment of Irreversible Processes (ICLATIP-30)
4th-7th Jan 2011, Kathmandu University, Dhulikhel, Nepal

Toward the South Pole was to be one of my most memorable vacations.

Shared a cabin with Ray Schwartz and his wife, Bethe, on the seafaring excursion.

Accompanying Bethe was a stuffed penguin that landed with us on King George's Island.

Here I ran a marathon videotaping my adventures on an uninhabited continent.

On a cold wintry morning in 2011

Where the rains pelted down from the heavens,

A lone penguin stood alongside the human packs

For a race across icy hills and muddy tracks.

Penny was her name, though she may in fact have been male.

But such was the fellowship that none did wail.

And why should there be when all were winners.

For the merry band of Antarctic marathoners.

On returning from my polar adventures, a devastating earthquake struck Japan.

The ensuing tsunami destroyed the Fukushima nuclear power plants.

Alongside Chernobyl, the worst nuclear disaster with widespread contamination.

At a time the world wanted to solve their energy crisis with fission.

If there are indeed silver linings to every storm cloud,

My radiation detector company profited from the radioactive fallout.

My original goal was to complete a marathon on all seven major continents.

Furry critters would now accompany me on this global accomplishment.

Penny the Penguin on Antarctica was the first of the marathon beasts.

Each animal would be synonymous with the land upon which they feast.

Before my next beastly conquest of another continent to face

I endured the glorious suffering of back-to-back marathon races.

Through our capital city I pounded the 26.2 miles in a decent time.

Followed next day by a marathon along the scenic Atlantic shoreline.

Was in a show hosted by John Bredin at the bookstore Symposia.

Public Voice Salon was televised on local cable network media.

There I met a colorful character, Gigi Olivieri, and her daughter Heidi.

Self-proclaimed sinner who found salvation through Christianity.

Gigi reminded me of another saved soul in Kitty Ragin.

The spirit of Christ blew away the evils before she could be taken.

And bonded by love, her husband Mike followed Kitty to redemption,

A former drug dealer to Richard Pryor, the world-famous comedian.

Kirstin and Chris were my connections to Mike and Kitty.

Fellow Globonders introduced by Tod Volpe.

Before Facebook brought true social networking to an end.

Instead of meeting real people, you now connect to virtual friends.

Next marathon beastly adventure was to be in China.

Pete the Panda would represent the continent of Asia.

My namesake brother was to tackle half the distance.

Along the historic wall I scaled with sweaty persistence.

In 2011 on the Yin and Yang Square

They came east and west for the marathon fair.

There was a brother and a panda named Pete.

To scale with Leong, the Great Wall, or be beat.

The circumstances allowed me to mix business with pleasure.

Asia was in panic over the Japanese nuclear disaster.

After the marathon I toured the region giving safety lectures.

Took the opportunity to promote my company's radiation detectors.

Both my personal and commercial lives are drawn inexplicably toward China.

To supply their demanding economy, they invested heavily into nuclear.

I expanded the business scopes on my continuing trips to China.

From selling products to seeking an investor partner.

Our goals were technology transfers for cash and commercial exposure.

My promotions did eventually spark a corporate takeover.

In Nepal I'd met the Vougioukli family from Greece.

With singing sisters that could charm Ares, the god of war, into peace.

They came to stay with me for an exploratory US visit.

Their beauty and talents got them several proposals of marriage.

Atop Mount Olympus they listened to their daughters.

Angelic goddesses serenading forgotten worshippers.

Eleni so fair and sweet of sonic voice.

Souzana plucking magical tones with elegant poise.

The wedding of Todd Allievi and Kexin Li was exaggeratedly memorable.

Hurricane Irene threatened to turn their special day into a debacle.

A last-minute change of venue allowed the ceremony to continue.

As the minister who gave the vows, I avoided further misfortune.

Scientifically proving the existence of GOD is merely the beginning.

Starting a new religion based on faith and proof would be defining.

Knowledge would be my bible, and truths my commandments.

Places of worship would also serve as educational establishments.

In the Republic of San Marino I gave a presentation on anti-antimatter.

From the duality of space-time will spring forth four particle vectors.

Normal matter can be interpreted as positive space moving forward in time.

Antimatter in the same positive universe is equivalent to a reverse timeline.

Hence, when matter and antimatter annihilate, they produce double the energy mass quanta.

But since their net time will cancel out to zero, the original particles will exist no longer.

And in the reverse negative-spaced universe is the presence of an identical pair of twins.

So anti-antimatter can be considered as negative space moving backward in a time spin.

Science relies on quantifying with our five physical senses that are observable.

To expel tricks and errors, all measurements must be reproducible.

Faith relies on the quality of our inner spiritual intuitions.

The devil can play wicked games with your sensitive emotions.

A rigorous proof with unwavering faith combines for the perfect argument.

Your mind and soul reunified to trumpet the only truthful testament.

GOD not only wants to be worshipped but wants to be seen to be worshipped

So that the devil's tricks will be exposed for all to demolish.

In science we seek true facts, cold and calculating.

In life we seek true love, warm and endearing.

But they are merely two sides of the fabric of existence.

Unbalanced souls look upon only one surface for veneration.

Love on its own cannot provide for physical exploration.

And neither can facts alone satisfy our spiritual sustenance.

On a memorable bright day in Berlin when records were broken freely

Makau's world was followed by bests from Kwabena, Kino, and Healy.

Bernie the Bear and his international entourage running brave and tall

Through the streets of a city once divided east and west by a great wall.

Men wear suspenders and shorts in Bavaria.

Also famous for Oktoberfest, a festive beer mania.

Busty fräuleins serving out liters of beer mugs under canvas tents.

Thousands of drunks with amazingly no brawling fights to contend.

Completed our marathon tours through Salzburg and Vienna,

Birthplace of perhaps history's most notorious character, Hitler.

Though his Nazi empire did not last a thousand years,

His murderous legacy will forever be sustained by millions of tears.

For North America marathon there were two qualifying beasts.

In size they spanned the extremes from largest to least.

Monty saluted the Stars and Stripes and Maple Leaf on crossing the border.

While Rudy accompanied superheroes across New York's five boroughs.

Across two nations sharing a common history of English

Monty the Moose trots from Buffalo to Niagara for a marathon finish.

A tired soul cheered by thunderous roars of the mighty falls.

With a magical rainbow mist at the end was the perfect call.

From the legacy of Fred Lebow, the world's greatest marathon did flower.

In a city once full of tears, rebuilding with a new Freedom Tower.

Crowds cheered Rudy the Rat as he scurried across five boroughs on tiny feet.

With a league of real superheroes protecting the liberty of even protesters on Wall Street.

If 2010 was a devilish madhouse culmination.

2011 concluded like a saintly monastic vocation.

China was my end-of-year destination.

Dual role of business and family vacation.

IN THE END

(2012)

Ancient civilizations predicted an end is near.

Future kind evolved to higher states will appear.

Natural selection is a brutal evolutionary arms race.

Where the strong victimize the weak to forward their genetic case.

Laws were formulated to control our biological longings.

Still in times of crisis we revert back to raping and pillaging.

To prosper, humanity must climb the next evolutionary branch.

A godly species linking new life onto the taxonomic rank.

2012 marks end of the Mesoamerican Long Count calendar.

Coincides with the winter solstice falling on 21st December.

In the prophetic wake of the Chinese year of the Dragon.

Unexpected happenings will follow this beast from heaven.

12-21-12 most powerful symbolism is related to its opposing dual nature.

Twin universes leads to a scientific proof of GOD that will truly inspire.

Sean John was seeking solace from a family drama.

Took him and others out west to Sedona.

Stayed at the Zen House managed by Larry Rosenberg.

There were Mike and Kitty who represented the established church.

Isabella Green, a beautiful Russian with spiritual vibes.

And best friend Martin, who will forever be by my side.

Through a late winter storm we drove to visit the Hopi Indians.

They foretell a changing future like their Mayan cousins.

Ruben Saufkie from Second Mesa was our guide to Prophecy Rock.

Inscribed on a monolith are dual paths for humanity's fated clocks.

One shows excess indulgences ticking to a rapid extinction.

Alternative passive way of life will lead to a longer existence.

Each was handed a feather for the closing ceremony.

Fate cast a shadow that will always be in our memories.

For upon that summit stood four who showcase the entire human race.

Martin placed his feather north to represent his white face.

Sean, of black heritage, laid his eagle's quill facing south.

Our red Indian host pointed west with sacred corn in his mouth.

As the yellow man from the east, I completed the compass.

But the real miracle was yet to be unveiled by the cosmic forces.

Focused my camera on the four feathers laid in front of the stone
of fortune.

A gush of wind would direct where our paths would be destined.

Though we set down our individual feathers pointing out in all
directions,

Heaven intervened to group our plumes toward the same orientation.

So the photograph I captured showed the human race must go in unity.

Parallel to the chosen paths on Prophecy Rock that came from the
Almighty.

Before sunrise we climbed up to Cathedral Rock to view the coming spring equinox.

With opened arms we greeted the first rays breaking over the summit rocks.

Our spiritual experiences would have a lasting legacy upon us.

Isabella decided moving permanently to Sedona was a must.

Next marathon beast saga was with Leo the Lion in South Africa.

Once more my faithful two-legged companion was Martin to run an ultra.

It had been over a decade since we were last on the Dark Continent.

Scaling Kilimanjaro, the world's highest free-standing mountain.

In Cape Town with Table Mountain as a beautiful background scenic.

Leo battles rain and hills as he crosses ocean waves from Indian to Atlantic.

5K international fun run on Good Friday alongside the Waterfront's tourist queues.

Rain gods blessed to cool the 56K ultra-marathon, though it clouds the iconic views.

I missed my eldest niece's wedding because it clashed with the Two Oceans Marathon.

So when my next niece in line wedded her dream man, it was double the fun.

The occasion reunited our family to long-missed relatives from Singapore.

We all have blossomed into richness from seeds laid in soils so poor.

The vestige of Fukushima continued to hang in the air like an exploding atomic mushroom cloud.

Compounding the global fears was Iran's nuclear research that Israel threatened to attack aloud.

For my profession this was the silver lining that raised our commercial image.

Shareholders, of whom I was one, accepted a buyout by Thermo Fisher Scientific.

With money in the bank and a new global sales position working out of my home office,

I invested in African Cape parrots named after a couple I connected with acting as Cupid.

Kino and Mayu were feathered companions in my new SkyClub apartment.

The place, owned by my brother who quit his Hong Kong corporate employment.

Pete decided to tour the world before returning to New York.

Our paths would cross in an upcoming marathon in an Aussie port.

Competing in an Ironman triathlon is the ultimate physical sporting endurance.

Entered with untrained trepidation New York's inaugural US Championship tournament.

Swam 2.4 miles along Hudson River toward George Washington Bridge.

Followed by 112 miles biking along Palisades Interstate Parkway rolling ridges.

Finished with a 26.2 miles marathon that was more walking than run.

Only at the end could I savor the triumphant accomplishment with fun.

My prophetic dreams had returned, which had me in awe.

Perhaps I was proving myself worthy of innocence once more.

A nightly vision showed me a 6–4 set for Murray over Federer in a tennis match, winner takes all.

Days before, the Scotsman won Olympic gold at Wimbledon over his rival with that exact final score.

Before my Ironman I'd a premonition of a time with 15 and 6 on the clock.

And, as predicted, I crossed the finish in 15 hours 53 minutes and 6 seconds on the dot.

I so wanted to tell others before the events of my visionary messages.

But recalled how I lost this godly gift as a greedy child seeking advantages.

August 11, 2012

Aquadraat
IRONMAN.
U.S. CHAMPIONSHIP

Official Time
15:53:06

2585

My life continued to prosper even though I was surrounded by chaos.

Civil wars in the Middle East infested their citizens with deathly pathos.

Global economic stagnation threatened social unrest and even revolutions.

And smart gadgets had overtaken religion for people's obsessive devotions.

Even as I write, this history of my life journey that has come full circle.

The story reflects humanity's next great cycle for eternal survival.

The words to follow are not of the past but the present and future.

Guided by a GOD who many abuse to commit wanton terror.

Where knowledge is my bible and truths are my commandments.

Do not do what I do, but do what I preach will be my gifting testament.

As a Westerner I have always considered democracy as our greatest virtue.

And Communism as the evil empire that kept their citizens under curfew.

Yet comparing the world's two largest populaces cast doubts on such propaganda.

Each government will only present one-sided facts for its own agenda.

With a quarter of the planet's humans living under China's single-party rule.

Its Asian neighbor and rival India with over a billion potential voting pool.

Both have similar geography and demography.

Sharing much of their spiritual culture and history.

China has by far out-competed all its main competitors.

Even in profiting from capitalism it has surpassed the Westerners.

And the old adage that its governing system breeds corruption

Sounds hypocritical when Wall Street bankers can cause a global recession.

Instead of judging the superficial, glossed-over surface,

Better to search within for the truthful message.

My fellow Brits complain about the weather conditions.

As do my fellow Yanks about our politicians.

This is the true worth of democracy.

The carefree opportunity to whine freely.

But in principle, a Communistic state could allow for such freedom.

By overcoming fears that dissensions will lead to a revolution.

Poverty and starvation are the predominant causes for social uprisings.

When people have full stomachs and toys to play, there is no desire for rebelling.

Though money cannot buy happiness, it can at least provide for contentment.

The system that generates prosperity for its citizens is therefore the best governance.

Before the unions, powerful owners abused their employees.

Child labor and slavish conditions used to maintain low salaries.

With the rise of the united workers came reverse exploitation.

Restrictive work practices made for uncompetitive production.

Ultimately, power is the worst form of corruption.

Whether from an individual or a collective union.

The same can be said of almost all human activities.

Unrestrained greed will overcome our empathies.

Magna Carta was the great chapter of medieval English liberties.

The Constitution the supreme law of United States democracy.

Giving free people innate legal rights from abuse.

And restricting excessive power from a tyrant to misuse.

Hence for righteous living there must be abiding fundamentals.

Principles defining explicit core values that must be adhered by all.

Unambiguous and logical that even an artificial intelligence can govern.

Those that maliciously stray must be punished with loss of their freedom.

First edict, thou must obey all decrees hence set forth.

No deviations or arguments will be permitted no matter the cause.

The logic is to unequivocally define what is right from wrong.

So your chosen paths clearly lay with petals or prongs.

Second edict, thou must accept a Single Omnipotent Consciousness, that of GOD.

Worship nothing or only one Supreme Being above all others in the religious path trod.

Speak no evil upon GOD nor take actions against those praying in the divine light.

All can give sermons, but none can give curse in GOD's name even in plight.

Third edict, thou must not end the life of another innocent soul.

Defend against harmful intent but seek no vengeance and let justice flow.

Slay without cruelty only what is essential to maintain one's sustenance.

Cherish all life and live to fulfill goodness in your own existence.

Fourth edict, thou must not steal others' possessions.

Neither their property, family, nor their creations.

Earn your values through your own inspiration and efforts.

Gifts taken should be repaid to others with kindness and comfort.

Fifth edict, thou must not take advantage of the weak.

Be they young, old, sickly, or meek.

Use your strength to build admiration.

And your courage to defy oppression.

Sixth edict, thou must respect others' distinctions.

Lead by example and not by coercion.

Diversity is the rainbow of life.

Evolution the colorful spice.

Seventh edict, thou must not bear falsehood.

Gains by untruths are unholy loot.

Present yourself with rightful facts.

And fear not any attacks.

Eighth edict, thou must not needlessly destroy.

All benevolent creations should be preserved to be enjoyed.

Do not vanquish what you dislike.

If it causes you no harm, then take a hike.

Ninth edict, thou must not conquer fruitful lands

If the natural inhabitants are opposed with their stand.

Take virgin grounds or desert plots for needed incursion.

Improve the worth of the land to justify the expansion.

Tenth edict, thou must seek knowledge for evolution.

Wisdom is to eternal creation what ignorance is to rapid extinction.

Govern by intellect should be the final decree.

Be conscious of humanity's delicate tree.

Laws of thermodynamics govern all sciences.

Energy is critical to drive our technological advances.

On the Greek island of Kos I was an invited presenter.

Giving lecture on Santilli's Hadronic nuclear fusion reactor.

Reconnected with familiar scientists and mathematicians,

Including Peter Rowlands, a fellow academic Liverpudian.

Santilli's Isodual theory predicts four time-dependent particle creations.

Akin to virtual vacuum fermions in Rowland's nilpotent predictions.

Nicely complimenting my own four matter states in twin universe existence.

Science is not merely heading toward a renaissance but a revolution.

Perhaps more profound is Erik Trell's biological implications.

That numeric geometries are building blocks of life's foundations.

The same fundamental shapes can also explain cosmic features.

Everything is interconnected, even between rocks and creatures.

The conference was a major success, highlighting Santilli's teachings.

From theoretical concepts to production prototypes and even commercial dealings.

Informed Ruggero and Peter I would ride on their scientific greatest.

On my own mission to experimentally prove existence of GOD to the masses.

Toured mainland Greece with the Vougioukli family.

Panoramic view of Mount Olympus, the home of ancient deities.

Visited tomb of Phillip II, father of Alexander the Great, located in Vergina.

And guided in the port city of Thessaloniki by beautiful Eleni and Souzana.

Just as the East builds its cultural history upon Chinese foundation,

So the Greeks can be considered the founders of Western civilization.

Philosophers such as Aristotle developed disciplined principles and logical thinking.

From literature, medicine, politics, and science that continue to impact our way of living.

The world is not enough for me.

This was told to me on my journey.

It so resonates with who I am.

And what it is I demand.

In a future utopia where laws are not needed.

Humanity governed by logic and godly edicts.

Evolution sustained by limitless energy pace.

Population expanding into endless outer space.

Labor is exercise and work is thinking.

Collective knowledge for higher evolving.

Tapping into the parallel reservoir of antimatter.

Where GOD resides as our ultimate instructor.

The more we know, the more we will need to discover.

It is the inner search where we are to be a destined explorer.

Turning chaos into order needs to reverse entropy.

Our godly twin universe will provide for the negative energy.

As we evolve to greater levels of awareness,

We come closer to the Single Omnipotent Consciousness.

The emotional pain of loss will become a thing of the past.

As unions of love in our combined universes will forever last.

Long into the future where human forms no longer exist

Will come a time when the division to GOD ceases to persist.

Our divine consciousness can then birth its own cosmic being.

And the eternal cycle of universal life will once more begin.

East and West will transition to new leaders with opposing
ideology.

Communism and Democracy jostling for global supremacy.

Hu Jintao replaced by National People's Congress as chairman.

Barack Hussein Obama to contest for second term as president.

My life is like a repeating fractal of the cosmic world.

With China and US battling for my devoted soul.

Even in the 2012 London Olympics I had divided loyalty

On neutral English soil that once supported my family.

Perhaps it is Britain that holds the ideal solution.

Roots for both the democratic system and the trade union.

Here the inventors of the Industrial Revolution started capitalism.

And workers collectively demanding equal rights under socialism.

Even in politics there is a uniquely quaint British sentiment.

Parliament consists of two chambers of the government.

House of Commons seated by democratically elected members.

House of Lords akin to Communistic-appointed upperclass fellows.

I greatly benefited from the free health care and education.

And in return, my family worked hard to pay back society through taxation.

A utopian system where citizens can be strong of body and mind.

Carefree to contemplate on what is truly spiritually divine.

But life is never so simple when humans are involved.

Not until a higher benevolent logical species has evolved.

As the civil war in Syria rains stray bombs onto Turkey,

The UK Met Office reports the wettest summer in a century.

Humanity is staging a two-front battle against itself and nature.

The outcome of both will only lead to a grim future.

Yet it is after mass extinctions that evolution flourishes anew.

At the end of the Permian era the numbers of survivors were few.

Dinosaurs became the dominant species for the next hundred million years.

Until a colliding asteroid ended their colossal reign of fear.

Mammals took over the ecological leadership.

And at the apex came Homo sapiens to take the controlling whip.

The major difference is we are now in a technological age.

Where brains have superseded brawn as the dominant gauge.

To evolve to a higher state means radical new minds.

So the next mass extinction can be intellectually confined.

With smart logic we can peacefully avoid irrational wars.

And correctly assess our greedy impact before the climate falls.

Losing the battle for our inner souls will suck us into a hellish void.

For the demons within can be more destructive than any bombarding asteroid.

An independent panel finally uncovered the truth on the Hillsborough disaster.

When ninety-six Liverpool football fans died during a FA Cup semi-final fixture.

For twenty-three years the fans were blamed by falsified police testimonies.

The prime minister apologized on behalf of the nation to the city and grieving families.

I'd dreamt my beloved team would win their nineteenth league title.

With their worst start for a century and a new manager it would be a miracle.

Perhaps my faith and loyalty is being put through a test of fire.

To prove whether I am indeed a trusted prophet or a stupid liar.

If my heart is so easily swayed by results of a sporting battle.

Then I am too weak a champion to fight for a holy struggle.

Maybe my weaknesses are really my greatest strength.

For I rebuke others that insist my self-image is immense.

They claim EGO stands for Edging GOD Out.

But I insist it is Ensuring GOD's Obedience that I tout.

A man tells Buddha "I Want Happiness," so the story goes.

Buddha said first remove "I," for that's your ego.

Then remove "Want," for that's your desire.

Now you are left only with "Happiness" to admire.

And these few words reflect the paradox of my conflicting life.

I do not want happiness, yet it seems from my adventures to be rife.

My true desire is total gratification that I am to be proven right.

But if I don't listen to my own wise words, then I will surely lose the fight.

The hard lessons in life that I've learned I put down in these words.

So others who read and understand can avoid going wayward.

The more righteous I am, the more fun and productive I've become.

To be good of mind, body, and soul is to be truly wholesome.

My mind is molded by studied education.

From intellectual masters such as Einstein and Newton.

Giving me the scientific tools to explain my twin universe.

As well as the foundation to succeed in commerce.

My body I put through physical tests.

Yet I am naturally lazy in training, I do confess.

Having good friends to work out is a blessing.

And racing in exotic places is motivating.

My soul has been the most difficult to enlighten.

Having a purpose at least gives direction to one's passion.

But there are no exams or medals to gauge your success.

Be resolute in faith and always try your virtuous best.

Essence of existence comes in three flavors that govern the cosmic destiny.

Be it the Father, Son, and Holy Spirit of the Trinity.

Or the number of quarks that make up the fundamental baryonic particles.

Even our own timeline consists of three phases that are discernible.

Past is captured in our mind as memory filaments.

Present is where our body exercises for life's elements.

Future is the direction our soul takes us on the path to our final union.

Be in heaven or on earth, we are interconnected by triple unification.

In KLYSTAR, even Leo's loving companions appear as three primary colorful maidens:

Tracy, of watery sapphire blue eyes, symbolizes the hero's past with loyalty that could not be shaken;

Neanna, with pupils of earthy emerald green, is synonymous with his present adventure-seeking character;

Suling's fiery ruby red stare seeks out a future beyond physical or mental bounds that all can master.

We even talk to our computers using a three-digit binary system.

Two is the fundamental base upon which all numbers are sequenced.

One represents a bit of information which the electronic circuit turns on.

Zero is the reverse "off" position with the electrons gone.

Two is also the base for the existence of twin universes.

Solutions to square root give a positive value and its negative inverse.

Hence the ultimate cosmic solution must have foundation in dualism.

Be it mental, physical, or spiritual, the nature of pairs is realism.

One is defined as the Single Omnipotent Consciousness,

GOD being the primary supercomputer of the universe.

The only natural value that retains its unique constancy.

Try to divide or multiply GOD, and you still get total unity.

Zero is representative of the unbreakable force of our godly nature.

Try to divide this value, and you will achieve infinite failure.

Nothing is also the sum of twin universes when all quantities are reversed.

Obeying the universal laws of thermodynamics that everything is conserved.

Pi is a mathematical constant for the ratio of a circle's circumference to its diameter.

It is also the secret code that contains within all the answers to nature.

The two diametric halves represent the opposing sides of our twin universe.

A single diameter is the one GOD that governs heaven and earth.

All is circumferentially enclosed by an infinite zeroing force.

The cyclic rhythm of our existence is set by this numbering course.

If life does indeed follow art, then my fictitious character Leo is leading me.

And as such, unnatural storms chase us both, no matter where we flee.

Century-only hurricanes to strike in consecutive years are indeed freaky.

Irene was followed by Sandy that left devastation in my home state of New Jersey.

Maybe the symptoms of global warming and nature's dissatisfaction.

Or worse, a cosmic warning and humanity's godly dissolution.

Yet even in the eye of a hurricane is a peaceful lull.

Stay within the center of the beast and we will not be culled.

Stray away from the heart and we will suffer stormy assaults.

An unforgiving flood can lead to deadly results.

My friend James Peck's death coinciding with the onslaught of Sandy was tragic.

A mathematical genius who coded algorithms to benefit operational logistics.

He was also a true believer of my twin universe from the beginning.

Unlike pretenders who get converted based on one's fame and mass followings.

It is right and proper to question what you do not understand.

But wrong to make judgments when an ignorant woman or man.

I shot a sequence of images of the damaging floods in Hoboken.

BBC posted my pictures and videos along with an interview by webcam.

Contaminated waters lingered for several days and power lost even longer.

Though the lands suffered greatly, it was a fast track for the majority to recover.

In large part because emergency planning and response was well executed.

By the government serving its people was why it succeeded.

A sad aftermath of the storm was the cancellation of New York marathon.

The race survived the terrorist attacks on 9/11 but not the damaging cyclone.

The problem was not logistics or safely but the objections of some sufferers.

They wanted their grief shared among the international field of runners.

Recalling when the doctor told me of my father's terminal illness, I was sad.

Seeing the physician enjoying life in the corridor with nurses made me mad.

I then realized that our personal anguish should be suffered alone.

Expecting a stranger to care about one's pains is not a way to atone.

Receiving blessings and comfort from others is desirable.

But do not demand rest of society to be equally miserable.

Lack of fuel and electricity was the main shortage.

Too many vehicles and corroded transformers caused outrage.

Centralized mass shelters and road transit are needed for a far worse disaster.

We can adapt efficient commercial supply chain logistics to provide the answer.

In a crisis situation, collective survival outweighs selfish requirements.

Nourishing and transporting en masse is more effective management.

In times of chaos you get to know who your true supporters are.

Who will stand loyally with you and who will scramble away far.

It's easy to be generous in giving to those you lust in times of plenty.

True tests come when your neighbors seek aid when conditions are nasty.

Matt McClelland came from afar to volunteer for cleanup duties.

Whereas a nearby acquaintance didn't care to invite us to their dinner party.

The natural beastly instincts are to be a selfish taker.

To be closer to GOD one must evolve into a generous giver.

I was requested at work to give a roadmap for a nuclear future.

Another twisted paradox of my life that I am not a true believer.

It is not the technology I fear but the beasts that use it.

Planning a strategy for when the atomic bombs tick.

I comfort myself that my business is on passive detection.

And not development of active release of deadly radiation.

Yet the assaulting storms have demonstrated nature is even more powerful.

Consequence of a catastrophic climate change makes humanity's survival doubtful.

With a blade we can kill a man, and a nuclear bomb can finish off millions.

Comparatively insignificant when global warming can devastate billions.

Around a hundred US lives did hurricane Sandy take.

Multiply by a thousand for those killed in 2008 Sichuan earthquake.

Double up for human losses in 2004 Indian Ocean tsunami.

And the 1931 China flood swept away over a million to join the Almighty.

Still these are all relatively localized, small-scale disasters in comparison.

A prolong worldwide collapse would be of true biblical proportions.

Over two billion dollars was spent on the US elections.

Ended with no change in president and congressional selections.

A democracy where votes are effectively paid for with money.

And negative attacks on opponents are endorsed as good policy.

I reluctantly voted because it felt like it was my duty.

For the first time ever I contemplated selecting a right-wing party.

Inside the voting booth I went with my usual liberal party line.

But felt no joy in going with the winning candidate this time.

Politics, like religion, must change for the better.

Otherwise people's disillusions will turn them bitter.

But changes tend to occur only after disastrous failures.

Or the coming of a Messiah to lead us to greener pastures.

China selected Xi Jinping as their new leader for a decade.

So East and West superpowers have bosses to debate.

Politics are polarized in opposite directions.

Economics bind them to self-serving cooperation.

On Four Mile Beach in Port Douglas we viewed a total solar eclipse.

Kylie the Kangaroo with Ying family watching the lunar dip.

Breaking sun signaled the start of a marathon extravaganza.

With the treacherous bump track, an uphill brutal meander.

Completed the Seven Continents Marathon mission.

Began with New York for the North American portion.

Europe was accomplished in London with the fastest time
to boast.

Racing across Rapi Nui, along headed moai off the South
American coast.

Penny the Penguin was the first of the accompanying marathon
beasts in Antarctica.

The Great Wall was perhaps the toughest challenge to tick off
Asia.

Africa achieved with the Two-Oceans Ultra-Marathon in
Cape Town.

Solar eclipse for Oceania completed the continental crown.

Rode upon a caravan of camels to view the sunrise over the
sacred Ayers Rock.

Uluru in the aboriginal's tongue that is told of the creation stories to their flock.

From prehistory to modern life we continued our adventures
onward to Sydney.

Climbed atop Harbour Bridge, the largest single-span arched
gateway for vehicular journeys.

The end of one journey is marked by the beginning of another.

But life can only flourish if the cyclic changes are major.

And that time of change is now upon me and the rest of humanity.

The course we choose will define our lasting legacy.

In the beginning there was innocent emptiness.

Learning to grow order from expanding chaotic wildness.

GOD is the ultimate singularity of conscious order.

Logic is our cold defining path to controlling power.

Love is the hot passion to drive our evolutionary creations.

In the end, to survive we must thrive to a godly reunion.

Is this to be My End or My Beginning?

Is this to be Our Start or Our Finishing?

The answers are already known throughout space and time.

It is the questions that we must correctly ask to find.